Reflections of a Cowboy

Steve Nestor

1st Edition, 2023 Reflections of a Cowboy.

Paperback (B&W): 978-1-7393242-0-9

Paperback (Colour): 978-1-7393242-4-7

Hardback: (B&W): 978-1-7393242-1-6

Hardback (Colour): 978-1-7393242-3-0

Ebook: 978-1-7393242-2-3

Book Cover and illustrations by Steve Nestor

Published by Nestor

Dedication:

This book is dedicated to my inspiration, the wonderful Mrs Nestor, and to Leah, Dan, Jack and Sam who make me proud every single day. Not forgetting the very special Louis, Melissa, and Alex who bring so much love and laughter to my life.

Reflections of some of my readers:

"Amongst the darkness we witness his immense courage, his profound strength and his utterly beautiful soul. Steve Nestor is a fucking hero" **Aimee Bateman**

"Reading Reflections of a Cowboy has helped me start a journey I really needed to start. I couldn't put it down, I was in pain for the author but at the same time I could hear the lesson he was teaching. I have identified areas that I need to work on to improve my life thanks to reading this book!" **Jacqui Mortimer**

"Steve's book provides that hopeful lift we all need sometimes. It doesn't profess to be a complex self-help book, but one that offers simple, reflective, easy to apply mental take aways that can be used in our daily lives." **Victoria Etchells**

"This is a book of hope, of inspiration, and of the profound role of having people in our lives who truly believe in us!" **Nick Cummins**

"This book made me more reflective than I have been in a long time. The authenticity of the book shouts from the pages and it just feels like a real person talking to real people in a very surreal life story! Steve's honesty and willingness to share his darkest of times in the hope of helping others shows that if you feel stuck, you are never stuck forever.

Everyone should read this book! It is real."
Hayley Grainger

"This book will help you to understand what you can do to calm or dispute the fears or self-doubts that are holding you back. Reflections of a Cowboy gave me belief and the ability of me, and the possibilities for me – should I choose to accept them." **Jo Mason**

Reflections of a Cowboy

The first word:

Reflections of a Cowboy is a book of hope for anyone who feels stuck, and for those who have ever believed that they're not enough.

Born in Stoke-on-Trent and now living in Wolverhampton, first-time author Steve Nestor reflects on his abusive childhood and shares the lessons he's learned in the hope that he will inspire others who have experienced trauma in their lives to find the strength to live a life on their terms.

Please be aware that due to the nature of Steve's story, this book contains graphic references to the sexual, psychological and physical abuse he was subjected to that some may find upsetting. The lived experiences that he shares are the memories of what he went through and the reactions and responses are Steve's alone. The story is told from his perspective to represent events as faithfully as possible. The actions that he has taken have worked for him but there is no guarantee or suggestion that if you decide to follow a similar path that the results will be the same for you. We all have our own window on the world, our own challenges, strengths, skills, talents, hopes and dreams and what works for one, will not necessarily work for another.

The reasons for Steve sharing his story are many, but seeking sympathy is not one of them. He's found that when he shares his experiences, very often the first thing that people say is that they're 'sorry' for what happened. He really appreciates that people care, but there are only two people in this world who need to be sorry for what happened. One of them is dead and the other seemingly has no intention of ever apologising. So he's come to the conclusion that putting his words down on paper to allow whoever needs to hear his story is the best way to make a difference to as many people as possible, without anybody feeling the need to apologise for something that they had no hand in whatsoever.

Steve wants you to be in control of when and how you take in his experiences. He wants you to be able to reflect in your own time on what you can take from his learnings. He wants you to take what you need from his reflections to help you move past whatever challenges and obstacles you may be facing without ever having to feel the need to tell him how sorry you are for what happened to him.

It's important to note that this book is intended to provide inspiration and offer hope and kindness. Steve is a qualified and experienced coach and Emotional Intelligence practitioner but is not a medically qualified mental health professional, therapist, or psychologist so if anything within this book triggers or affects you in any way, please seek out the advice and support of the relevant professionals so that you get the help that you deserve.

You are an individual, so embrace your uniqueness and use the thoughts, ideas and experiences shared within the following pages and mould them to suit you. Use them as sparks to start your own fire.

Contents

1. Start from where you are 1

2. We're here for the blink of an eye.. 5

3. Reflect; On your challenges and success.............. 15

4. We always have a choice 18

5. We all have hopes and dreams 26

6. Your past does not define you.. 40

7. I'm a survivor (no I'm not) 60

8. Life is ACE (or is it?).. 70

9. I still feel sad at times 83

10. Believe; In endless possibilities.. 94

11. Be the person you always knew you were.......... 100

12. Allow yourself to live 105

13. What is happiness anyway?.. 114

14. The Invisible Man.. 148

15. Give a little respect (to yourself) 169

16. Different faces for different places..................... 176

17. Grow; Into the very best version of you 182

18. Ride for the brand 190

19. Celebrate the little wins 205

20. Are you in? 218

21. Life isn't a straight line 223

22. Your future is still unwritten............................. 231

23. Everybody needs a Mrs Nestor......................... 259

Reflections of a Cowboy

#ReflectBelieveGrow

"Look out for the things that make your heart sing. Recognise when you are smiling. Take note of when you lose yourself. Embrace all the good that life has to offer. Breathe those moments in and hold them in your mind."

Steve Nestor

1. Start from where you are

It was 1980 when he came into my life and more than 40 years later he still has a grip on me.

I've spent years stuck in my own head, paralysed by self-sabotaging thoughts. I allowed the parasitic seeds he planted during the six years of sexual, psychological and physical abuse to take root in my mind. Too often I compared myself to 'perfect' people including colleagues, managers, friends, family, celebrities or social media connections. I've wondered how they have 'got it together' when I feel like I'm falling apart. I've found myself asking questions like, how are they so confident in front of a room full of people, when I find myself having a mini-heart attack when I'm asked to introduce myself to a couple of individuals. And how do they have the guts to ask for 'more' when I'm questioning whether I'm worth the little that I have been given.

But I've realised over the years that what we very rarely see is that most of us are struggling with similar challenges. My experience of coaching people has shown me that regardless of your status, history, the amount of money you have, your age, gender, sexual preference or anything else you can think of, we all have our very own Kryptonite(s) that eat away at our confidence, resilience, self-belief and self-worth.

And in sharing my personal Kryptonites and leaving myself wide open and completely vulnerable throughout this book, I'm hoping that you will take something away that will help you to believe in yourself, respect yourself, and value yourself a little more. And that you find the motivation to move a step closer to being the very best version of you.

We all have a past, and it's down to us how we decide to use our experiences moving forward. Whatever has happened, has happened, and we can either choose to experience it as something to hold us back, or something to learn and build from. We all have our very own 'window on the world', but it is flawed. We see life through a filtered lens. Every interaction we've ever had, every news story we've ever heard, every book we've read, person we've met, song we've listened to, film we've watched, café we've been to, pub we've drank in, holiday we've been on, job we've done, and classroom we've sat in has contributed to creating our very own view of the world.

We very often only see what we want to see, and we find what we are looking for. In other words, if we believe that we are not enough or that we are stuck, we will always find things in our world that will confirm that to us.

As you turn the pages on my life so far you will see that although the lasting effects of the abuse that I suffered will never completely leave me, I've managed to take some positives from the rubble of my childhood and use them as the foundation to living a life on my terms where flourishing is now my norm.

If you allow it to, this book will:

- Offer hope
- Empower you to see the reality of your world
- Be your friend when you need a hug or shoulder to cry on and someone to listen to you
- Help you to silence the disempowering noises in your life
- Be your cheerleader, encouraging you to step towards living a life on your terms
- Help you to peel back the protective layers that you may have built around yourself over the years
- Be a mirror that helps you to see the real you
- Walk by your side every step of the way
- Be there whenever you need it
- Help you to see that you are (more than) enough
- Show you that you are in control and are not stuck.

I've written this book in the hope that my reflections bring value and hope to you, inspire you to believe in yourself and support you if you are in a position where you need a friend and a little kindness. Life is a series of stepping stones. We stay on some stones longer than others, we contribute more when we're in some places, and take what we need from others before hopping onto the next stage in our life. Where you are now, is not where you'll always be. Sometimes we just need reminding of that.

This book tells my story, but it is all about you.

Please take what you need and own it.

2. We're here for the blink of an eye

"No matter what people tell you, words and ideas can change the world." Robin Williams

When was the last time you watched the sun rise? I mean, really watched that huge ball of fire in the sky slowly grow on the horizon. And when you were watching it, how deeply did you think about the new day and the endless possibilities that potentially lie ahead of you?

I was on holiday in January 2023 in the Canary Islands with my wife and youngest son and read that the island we were visiting is 20 million years old, just think about that for a second. The sun has risen without fail over the black volcanic rocks in that beautiful place every single day for 20 million years. But the sun had been busy long before Fuerteventura was born. For more than 4.6 billion years the sun has been a constant in our skies. That's 4,600 million years!

Those kinds of timescales are hard to comprehend and the reason I've shared them is because when I was standing on the beach, silently watching the sunrise with the ocean tickling my toes, it further compounded my belief that many of us spend too much time in our heads; overthinking, not believing in ourselves, stressing and worrying about things that, in the big scheme of things, don't matter a jot. We're only here for the blink of an eye so what stops us from making the most of every single second?

I'm not a millionaire, a high-flying entrepreneur, an award-winning actor, a World Cup winner, or an Olympic medallist. I'm a middle-aged man who has experienced my fair share of challenges and have come through the other side, discovering my own version of happiness, success and contentment along the way. And if you'll allow me to, I'd like to share some of my thoughts, experiences and reflections with the aim of bringing hope, inspiration and kindness wherever it may be needed.

This book is for anyone who has ever felt stuck or feels that they're not enough and the reasons for writing it will become clear as you turn the pages on my life so far. And if you take nothing else from my reflections, please always remember that you are not stuck. You have the power to move from where you are and how you're feeling. If you choose to.

We are emotional, complex creatures and at times life can feel messy, difficult, confusing, and well, a bit rubbish really. It's easy to get stuck in our own heads, paralysed by self-sabotaging thoughts and beliefs. Our minds love to play tricks on us. We believe the stories we tell ourselves, and the ones we've been told about ourselves, and replay them in ways that are not always the most helpful. We live by rules that we don't remember setting and believe that it's 'just who we are.' We look for things that confirm the way we think; often pushing ourselves into a corner and justifying why we don't deserve better; why we're not worthy of living a life on our terms, a life that's meaningful and fulfilling, a life where we're our true self, a life where we are flourishing. But do you know what, it doesn't have to be that way. Believe it or not, what we think, isn't always the way it actually is.

What to expect

I like to keep things as simple as possible and to be upfront about what you can expect, so throughout the book I'll reference just a few ideas, models, frameworks (call them what you will) that I use, some of which I've developed myself, to help me to live a life where I finally feel like I'm flourishing and that I use to remind myself that I am enough. Over the following pages I'll share how I put these ideas into practice and towards the end of the book you'll find further details and exercises to work through if and when you feel they'd be helpful. Keeping all that in mind, everything I'll share stems from eight words that my wife said to me when we first met around 20 years ago:

"Choose to experience it in a different way."

Tracy Nestor (née Green)

Easier said than done but that one sentence has helped me to look at life differently and I've been practising this on a regular basis ever since. Often we can't control the events that go on around us and that affect our lives, but having worked on this over the years, I truly believe that we have complete control over how we respond to them, which has a direct effect on what happens in our lives.

This book is loosely structured around my Reflect, Believe, Grow framework which helps me to continuously learn and move forward with my life and ties in with my purpose. We will talk about the importance of meaning and purpose a little later in the book, but for now I'll just say that after a lot of work on myself I've discovered that my purpose is to;

Stimulate Reflection, Inspire Belief, and Ignite Growth to enable myself and those around me to flourish.

Quotes

You will find a spattering of quotes within these pages too, some of which are from comedians. And my reason for using quotes from the world of comedy is that humour, in all its forms, is so powerful and has been my 'go to' throughout my life. The ability of comedians to make even the most mundane tasks or darkest experiences funny, fascinates and inspires me in equal measure. If they can see things so differently to the rest of us and make us laugh out loud at things we'd usually cry at, ignore or just do mindlessly, how might I be able to change the way I think about my life?

I'd encourage you to take the time to think about what the quotes mean to you. Too often we see inspirational words sprinkled throughout the pages of books or on social media and our eyes quickly scan past them without allowing our brains to process the depth of meaning behind them.

As I mentioned earlier, one of the aims of this book is to be a friend when you need one; and good friends (in my experience) give you the time and space to think about things. They help by challenging you to see things from another perspective, and they empower you to make sense of the world around you. So please, if you're investing your precious time in reading through my reflections, ensure that you get the most value out of each and every word printed within these pages.

I'll warn you now that there may be more quotes from one person than any other, that is the one and only Billy Connolly. For as long as I can remember I have loved everything about him and I'll talk in a bit more detail later in the book about the positive influence he has had on my life. To start you off, I'll share one of my favourite quotes by him, and one that I remind myself of regularly.

"There's no such thing as bad weather, just the wrong clothing. So get yourself a sexy little raincoat and live a little." Billy Connolly

For me this quote directly ties back to the idea of choosing to experience things in a different way and underpins much of my thinking. There are some things we can do absolutely nothing about, but we always have a choice about how we'd like to respond. Having spent years hiding beneath a huge, boring beige umbrella, I'm finally ready to grab my very own 'sexy little raincoat,' and I hope this book will encourage you to join me. Maybe we can dance in the rain together one day.

You will also find a few 'cowboy' quotes (obviously, given the title of the book), and quotes from people I've met who have had an influence on my life. There are moments in time that can shape us, and I'm a great believer that we cross paths with people for a specific reason. That reason isn't always obvious at first but, if we choose to notice and act upon those moments, they can bring a richness to our existence and make a huge difference to us as individuals in our personal quest to live a life on our terms.

"I do what I do because I love making people smile." Rosanna Mastropaolo

It's now that counts

According to Julie Andrews, starting from the beginning is a 'very good place to start' but, maybe controversially to the Sound of Music[1] fans amongst you, I wouldn't necessarily agree. As I write I'm in my 52nd year on this planet and 'the beginning' seems a very long time ago for me, and not all that relevant to where I am now.

We have a magnet on our fridge that reads; 'How we spend our days, is how we live our lives.' The past is gone, all we have is the here and now, this very moment. Now that's gone, and again, and again; arguably, we don't even have now. The split second it takes between you seeing, feeling, tasting, smelling, or touching something, and the thought registering in your mind, means that EVERYTHING is in the past. Don't worry, this book isn't going to be a deep, philosophical read about the complex issue of consciousness, but what we will be doing is exploring how you could begin to make the changes that will help you to live a life on your terms; a life full of meaning, where flourishing is the norm.

I'm not a big fan of 'quick-wins.' In my experience anything offering you a shortcut to success, in whatever guise that takes for you, very rarely delivers what it promises. A few lines ago I mentioned that this book is loosely structured around my Reflect, Believe and Grow coaching framework and if you take the time to think about how the ideas shared relate directly to you, by the time you reach the back cover, you'll hopefully have your very own bespoke, 'you' shaped blue-print for living a happier, healthier, meaningful life.

To make any kind of sustainable change takes time, effort, and commitment so to ensure you give yourself the best possible chance of making the changes you've been thinking about, please answer this question honestly:

On a scale of one to ten (ten being 'bring it on' I'm ready to put in the work), how ready are you to commit to challenging yourself and making a change?

If you scored yourself an eight, nine or ten then brilliant, you're ready to go. Any lower, ask yourself what you need to do (or stop doing) to get to the point where you are fully committed to change. What could you take from this book that will help you? What's getting in your way? What needs to be different?

Why Reflections of a Cowboy?

Before we get into the book proper, I just wanted to share why I chose Reflections of a Cowboy as the title. As you can see from the cover image, I had a cowboy outfit way back when I was a little boy and maybe that influenced my love of all things 'Wild West', or maybe it was growing up watching John Wayne and Clint Eastwood films on the telly.

Whatever it was, I've always had a slight fascination with cowboys and a few years ago I discovered the Code of the West[2] and since then I've lived my life with these principles in the back of my mind. I'll make the odd reference to them as we go through the following chapters, sharing how they have helped me to overcome the challenges I've faced and to stay focused on what's important to me. If you like, they've been a driving force in my adult life, much like the cowboy who 'drives' the cattle through all weathers. Silently living by these principles has continuously helped me to move forward regardless of what's been in front of me. The inscription on John Wayne's headstone, star of numerous Western movies acts a reminder and source of inspiration to me whenever I find myself struggling to move forward. Hopefully it will help you too.

"Tomorrow is the most important thing in life. Comes into us at midnight very clean. It's perfect when it arrives, and it puts itself in our hands. It hopes we've learned something from yesterday."

John Wayne 1907-1979

3. Reflect; On your challenges and success

"The reason I talk to myself is because I'm the only one whose answers I accept." George Carlin

This book has been loosely arranged into three sections to match the framework that I've created and work with to ensure that I'm feeling the way that I want to feel for as much time as possible. But this is not a structured, clinical, 'how to' book. As humans we are complex creatures and, I don't know about you, but my brain doesn't always work best when I'm trying to fit my thoughts into neat little boxes, or creating tick-lists of top tips. I could have written a book that listed my experiences in chronological order and created a 'how to' of overcoming a traumatic childhood, but that didn't feel right.

I've gone around in circles trying to decide how best to structure this book so that you can get the most from it. I toyed with sharing my childhood experiences in the opening chapters, then explaining how I've dealt with them over the years but that wasn't right either. Mainly because, if I'm totally honest, I don't think I'll ever be in a position where I'll be able to confidently share that I have totally dealt with them. You'll see throughout this book that although I've come a long way, I'm still a work in progress in many ways, so it felt right for me to jump between experiences from my past and present to show how the things I've experienced in my life have affected me, and continue to influence my thoughts and actions.

I think that this is important to share because all too often we're shown the 'perfect' ending, the classic 'rags to riches' stories that can be inspiring. But I've found these to be demoralising at times and they have left me feeling even more inadequate and trapped in my problems. For that reason I've tried to create something that is relatable to anybody who feels stuck, anybody who needs a lift, and anybody who needs a little kindness. Hopefully my reflections will show that you don't have to fit into conventional little boxes to be happy and successful. You just need to define your own version of happiness and success, and commit to taking the small steps you decide are needed to help you live a life on your terms.

"We live the life we make, not the life we're given." Aimee Bateman

"Life is just a series
of moments to experience,
to enjoy whenever possible,
and to learn from."

Steve Nestor

4. We always have a choice

"If you find yourself in a hole, stop digging." Will Rogers

I'm a great believer that we always have a choice. Regardless of what's going on around us, we can decide how we'd like to respond. We can choose to walk away from an argument or decide to start a fight. We can react to bad news by telling ourselves that it is 'the end of the world', or we can respond by putting it into perspective and look for glimmers of positivity to hang on to. We can learn valuable lessons from our most challenging experiences or opt to use those events as reasons for not moving forward. Very often though we don't consciously make these decisions. Rather than taking a breath, thinking it through and responding, we revert to type and simply react, allowing our emotions to take control of us.

How many times have you heard people (yourself) saying things like; 'I'm just an angry/ jealous / anxious (insert any other emotion here) person' 'It's who I am, I can't help it.'? Can we get one thing straight here; you are NOT your emotions. Emotions are very often fleeting moments that we experience in response to events that are happening around us. They are a natural, normal part of being human. All emotions are valuable and to say that we need to push them aside and not 'feel' them would be a mistake.

It's important to understand that when an emotion 'knocks on your door' you always have a choice. Do you let it in, or do you treat it like an unwelcome door-to-door salesman, and say, 'not today, thank you'? I understand that it's easier said than done, but for the moment I simply wanted to plant the seed in your consciousness that you (and only you) are in control of the way that you feel.

I understand because for years I did not take control of my emotions. Negative thoughts consumed me, they had well and truly taken hold, my self-worth was rock bottom and I had zero confidence. I lived my life in a bit of a trance. I felt hollow and worthless. Even when I was shown friendship or affection it didn't mean anything to me. I look back now and feel sorry for the people in my life at that time as they weren't always treated in the best way and they never got to see the 'real' me. They only knew the person that I thought I was. I'm not proud of some of the things that I did back then, and since I've taken control of my emotions, I've revisited some of those times in my mind with fresh eyes and realise how little responsibility I took for myself. Always blaming others, expecting more, and waiting for happiness (we'll discuss happiness in more detail later in the book) to drop into my lap, or to be given to me by those around me. I know now that it was always there, inside me, just waiting to be uncovered.

I don't remember much about my early years. I know that I lived in Scotland for a while and my dad was in the Royal Navy, based in Helensburgh. I remember having a toy pedal car, a Rupert the bear Space Hopper, and a cowboy outfit. I remember my dad not being around much. When he left the navy he went to work on the oil rigs. One time he brought a drilled piece of rock home for me. It was about six inches across and a couple of inches thick with a circular rim, so smooth in contrast to the rough top and bottom, where a plethora of tiny fossilised creatures could be seen. I loved that piece of rock and spent hours studying it, running my fingers over the tiny shapes. But I can't for the life of me think where it went. A bit like my childhood really.

When I was about eight-years old I remember my mum and dad having a row in the kitchen. There was a bit of shouting and the next thing I knew my mum had a trickle of blood running from a cut above her eye. Even then I liked boxing and the injury reminded me of the kind of nick that a fighter would get. I later found out that she had 'banged' it against the fridge. I don't remember seeing my dad in the house again after that day but I did see him a couple of weeks later in town. I was on the bus and he was walking towards the local swimming baths which I later found out that he was using the showers there as he had nowhere to stay. I'd been told he was the bad guy so I ducked down so as not to be seen as the bus passed him. I wasn't to see him again for another fifteen years.

It wasn't long after my dad left that he moved in. He, otherwise known as Alan (we used his middle name as his first name was Peter, which was the same as my dad's) was my mum's new boyfriend. It was 1980, I was nine-years-old and my life was about to change forever.

I don't exactly recall when or even how it began. What I do remember is the searing pain that I felt as he assured me that 'it hurts more as a grown up so best to get it out of the way while you're still young'. My face buried into the soft white pillow, my cries muffled, my eyes closed but still leaking. Clinging onto the heavy brown and beige woollen blanket with my fingers and toes. Gripping it like a baby chimp clinging to its mother until it was over and my neck was released from his rough, nicotine stained fingers.

I don't remember ever feeling important despite his whisperings that it was our 'special secret'. The scratching of his rough sandpaper stubble against my soft freckle-spattered cheeks and the stench of stale beer and Park Drive cigarettes on his hot, desperate breath suggested to me that these were not special moments.

At the time I wasn't sure what they were or why I was being hushed out of bed in the middle of the night. My eyes stuck together with sleep. So tired that I bumped my way through the house, scraping my arms on the sharp swirls of Artex that had been used on virtually every wall. I just knew that I could tell nobody or 'something bad would happen'. He totally destroyed my childhood and extinguished my spark of innocence that I have desperately wanted back ever since.

His crushing of me coincided with Margaret Thatcher's reign as Prime Minister. Her destruction of the country was the backdrop to my abuse. Bobby Sands died in the Maze prison, starving himself to death in a bid to get his plea noticed. Maybe this could have been an option for me too? The Falklands War began when I was ten years old. The Battle of Goose Green started the day before my eleventh birthday and ended a day later. The British won the battle and, a few weeks later, the War.

That day I sat cross-legged on my bedroom floor. My favourite coach, horses and cowboy figures by my side. I was playing with my new Matchbox Race and Chase Scalextric set. A controller in both hands, my brain split between catching the criminal and escaping the blue and white American police car. Although my eyes were focused on the track, my ears were trained to listen for every creak on the stairs. 'Please not today'. I hoped to avoid my own battle, one that I knew I could never win. Even on my birthday there was no escape. My toys lay silent as he satisfied his needs.

The abuse continued, and a couple of years later whilst my coal mining uncles were fighting for their rights on the picket lines, I was still feeling as lonely and as scared as I did on that first time that he invaded me. The pain was still intense but at least I had the weekends to look forward to.

Saturday afternoons were spent with my Grandparents and Dickie Davies' World Of Sport. The coal fire was always crackling away and Grandma seemed to have an endless supply of Viscount biscuits and two fingered Kit Kats. Grandad would sit in his favourite armchair wearing his best tie and braces, reading the Daily Mirror's racing pages. I would always watch On the Ball presented by Brian Moore until the horse racing came on. That was my cue to go outside and inspect the giant leeks and check on the chickens in the warm and smelly coop at the end of the garden until it was time for the likes of Big Daddy, Giant Haystacks and Kendo Nagasaki to do battle in the wrestling ring.

I felt safe and loved. There was nothing to fear there. No creaking stairs or hushed threats. No nicotine-stained fingers and evil, piercing eyes. My Grandparents, uncles, aunts, cousins, and friends were all unaware of the ordeal that my life had become. I wished that my mum had also been unaware.

After years of silence I finally found the courage to tell her what had been happening. Her response still shocks me to this day, especially as I have children of my own. She did nothing. In fact she turned a blind eye and allowed him to continue to sexually, psychologically, and physically abuse me. I am still in contact with my mum. I don't know why, she brings nothing to my life and our relationship was irreparably damaged when she betrayed my trust. I suppose that I have learned to rise above the feelings of hatred and anger. My innocence was taken away and my childhood ruined but I have learned that getting stuck in the past will bring no good to my life. I must concentrate on today and look forward to the future.

Her reaction when I told her about the abuse confirmed to me that he had been right all along when he had said; 'Don't tell anybody or something bad will happen.' I now knew that I was alone. If my mother, the person who gave birth to me, who is supposed to protect me, was willing to allow this to happen then there was nobody to turn to. I would just have to put up with the abuse until I could leave. I was too scared, too tired, and too drained to do anything else.

Two years later he left. I didn't know why, and I didn't care. I couldn't see the point in asking. All that mattered to me was that I was 15-years-old and for the first time that I could remember I didn't go to bed worried that I may be woken up with a slap across the head, a punch in the small of the back, or something worse. The knot in my stomach that had been wound so tightly over that last six years remained for at least the next fifteen.

I was 30-years-old when I met Tracy, my now wife, and it was only then that my confidence began to grow and the knot of fear and mistrust began to untangle

5. We all have hopes and dreams

"Somewhere there's a score being kept, so you have an obligation to live life as well as you can, be as engaged as you can." Bill Murray

In the last chapter I gave a brief description of what happened to me during my childhood. As you can imagine, this is just the tip of the iceberg as it's impossible to distil six years of abuse into around fifteen hundred words. I wrote that passage as part of my creative writing course when I was studying with the Open University and it was the first time that I'd ever put pen to paper about what I'd been subjected to. I was forty-years-old when I wrote it and recalling some of the things that I'd been through affected me more than I thought they would and made me realise that I still had a way to go to be 'okay' with who I was and what had happened. I'd spoken about my abuse to many people but writing it down somehow made it more real, it brought it back into focus and helped me to see how far I'd come, but also how much I'd hidden deep within myself. When I'd told people my story I'd been called inspirational, and I suppose this made me believe that talking about it was all I needed to do to show that I was over it. But as you will know if you've experienced any kind of trauma, particularly as a child, it's never that easy.

Throughout this book I'll reference my abuse and lived experiences, going into more detail where relevant, but as I intimated earlier, I think it is more helpful to 'start from where you are' and decide where you would like to be, rather than to constantly go back to the beginning, or if not the very beginning, to a time when things went 'wrong' for you.

My passion for coaching comes from my belief that we all have the potential to live the kind of life that we choose to. We all have strengths, skills and talents, but not everybody feels like they have the opportunity to use them, to grow them and to improve on them. As was the case with me, too many people are waiting for somebody else to make them happy, to give them an opportunity, or to give them 'permission' to be themselves.

I mentioned how meeting my wife when I was thirty was a catalyst for change, and the last twenty years or so have seen many changes for me. I've gained a degree, I've spoken at national events on the power of storytelling, delivered countless sessions on the impact that having a positive mindset can have, and I've transformed myself from 'invisible' (that's how I often thought of myself) to a confident coach and mentor inspiring others. And all because my wife empowered me to believe in myself.

A good friend of mine, the wonderful Kelly Joynes, said to me at a mentoring celebration event we both attended in June 2022, that to help people to see their value, build their confidence, and to reach their goals it's becoming more obvious that it simply boils down to having someone believe in you. And I couldn't agree more.

For those who know me, you'll understand how much I adore Mrs Nestor. She was (and still is) my inspiration. Although she'll say that she did nothing, Tracy was the first person in my life to give me a chance. Where others had ignored, not noticed, or scoffed at my hopes and dreams, Tracy actively encouraged me to follow them.

When we first met I talked about how I enjoyed drawing and being creative, and a week or so later she'd paid for a cartooning course for me. I couldn't believe it, it was the first time that anyone had been bothered about what I wanted. I asked why and she simply said, "It's something you want to do, so why not?" When I'd finished the course I mentioned it to Lee who I worked with at the time and he said that he had a friend who had contacts in Hong Kong who were always looking for ideas for new ranges of collectibles. I was put in touch with him and a couple of weeks later I had decided on creating a range of cute kangaroos and was sketching ideas out for the collection which we (we being Tracy and I) called The KangaCrew. The family of 25 cute kangaroos fell into three categories.

'I Love Roo' including You're my world, Opposites Attract and Stuck on you. 'HeRoos' including a lifeguard, nurse, policeman, sailor, soldier and teacher, and 'Sporting HeRoos' including a footballer, basketball player, boxer, ice hockey player, golfer and, of course, a rodeo rider.

The designs were taken out to Hong Kong and a manufacturer out there liked them so much that they took the ideas on. The next couple of months were so exciting as we watched my drawings come to life. We were sent regular email updates and we saw them go from flat images to real life figurines. And when we received our very own set of figures I couldn't believe that the things that I'd thought of, sketched and drawn had made it into the world as actual touchable objects. I was so excited, so when I was told that the collection was being taken to the Hong Kong Gift Fair I started to dream that The KangaCrew would help to change my life and put me on the road to making a living through my creativity.

Unfortunately it wasn't to be. Although they generated lots of interest on their two visits to the gift fair, nobody wanted to take a chance on The KangaCrew at that point in time. I was gutted and all of the excitement and hope that had built up popped like a balloon, leaving me feeling deflated and back at square one.

But when I reflect, I wasn't back at square one at all. Things had begun to shift. That cartooning course had given me the opportunity to use my creativity and put my ideas and drawings in front of people who actually liked what I'd done. But because the disappointment was so great at the time I didn't celebrate that achievement, I only saw the negatives. I saw the rejection and focused my attention there. I now recognise that that was the first big turning point for me. I look at The KangaCrew most days and they act as a reminder that I created something that others felt worthy of bringing to life and they'll always have a very special place in my heart. Although they weren't a commercial success when I designed them I've never given up hope on the idea of them making their way into peoples' lives at some point in the future. I've got a few ideas in the pipeline for fiction novels and a couple of children's stories that I've been sitting on for a while. One of which is centred around the lives and adventures of my cute kangaroos so watch this space. The KangaCrew aren't a success… yet.

As well as my love for being creative, I told Tracy how I'd left school with just two 'O' levels and how I felt I wasn't capable of bettering myself. And within a few years she'd helped me to believe that I may have more to offer, encouraging me to study with the Open University which resulted in me graduating six years, 48 essays, and over 100,000 words later, at the age of 44 with a First-Class Honours Degree. Who knew I was capable of that? Tracy did. She has always believed in me which has resulted in me finally believing in myself, and hopefully my reflections will help you.

All of us have hopes and dreams, but not everybody takes the opportunity to fulfil them. Every one of us has skills and talents, but very often we're not given (or don't take) the chance to use them. We all have an idea of how we'd like to live our lives, but many of us never create the time and space to follow up on these thoughts.

I've had a colourful career (that's a creative way of saying that I've had loads of jobs), and one of my most fulfilling roles was as a support worker. Working with care leavers, the homeless, ex-offenders, people with drug and alcohol challenges, people living with mental ill health, and adults with learning disabilities to maintain their tenancies, find work, manage their finances and build their social connections. Although I'd never heard of the

GROW model[3] back then I took a coaching approach to my work as a support worker, it just seemed the natural thing to do. Who am I to decide what is best for anybody? I haven't lived their life, thought their thoughts, or felt their emotions. So asking what they wanted, helping them to work through their challenges, to focus on their strengths, and to decide their best way forward came completely naturally to me.

I truly believe that given the chance, we can all make the decisions that will lead us to wherever we choose to be, and now that I've realised this, my intention is to empower as many people as possible to believe that they can live a life on their terms. A happy, fulfilled, joyful, meaningful life where flourishing is the norm.

As a coach I understand that regardless of who you are, the position you may hold in an organisation, and how 'successful' you may seem to the outside world, we all have our challenges and insecurities. I love working with people and groups from all walks of life but I particularly enjoy working with individuals and groups who may never have been given the opportunity to be coached. Those people who may believe that they're not worthy of a better life, those who may have only ever been told that they're 'useless' or 'not good enough', those who can't see another way, and those who believe that 'this is it.'

I've been there and it's not nice. And I've worked with enough people for whom these feelings are their norm to know that there's so much potential out there, and sometimes all it takes is a little belief for it to be untapped.

In the words of Chesney Hawkes (look him up if you don't remember him) – you are 'the one and only.'[4] Your unique 'window on the world' is what makes you, you. Only you have experienced all the things that have happened to you. Nobody else has the exact same experience of life as you. How special does that make each and every one of us?

How many times have you watched one of those 'arty' films where there seems to be no ending; you know the ones that suddenly finish and the credits roll up in silence leaving you wondering why you'd just wasted the last two hours of your life on something that made no sense. Only to find out later that the same film had been nominated for numerous awards. What had they seen that you hadn't? Why did they think it was worthy of an award, and you just didn't get it?

The same principle applies to sport. For example, the introduction of Video Assisted Refereeing (VAR) means that there are so many cameras around the pitch in the top football leagues nowadays that the action can be watched from a whole host of angles. It can be rewatched, slowed right down, sped up, zoomed in on, and mathematical equations added to work out angles. So why are there still so many debates about whether the player was offside, whether it was handball, should it have been a red card, yellow card, or even a booking at all? We're watching the same thing and we all have access to the same images. But we all have our own very unique way of understanding the world around us and of interpreting the things that are put before us; which leads us to seeing things as we are, and not necessarily as they actually are. I first read the wonderful Reasons to Stay Alive, by Matt Haig[5] a number of years ago and have re-read it a couple of times since, and one of the many pearls of wisdom that he shares is that;

"There is no standard normal. Normal is subjective. There are seven billion versions of normal on this planet."

I love this. Who are any of us to say what 'normal' is? My 'normal' is very different to yours, but it's no better or worse. And as long as I'm happy with that, what's the problem? Well, in my opinion, there is no problem as long as the 'normal' you're living to is the real one!

I'll explain. For years I was told that I was worthless, pointless, useless, and thick and that I'd never be anything. My only uses were to be a punch bag, an object to tie up and violate, a thing that scraped the limescale off the toilet bowl, a bath-running, shoe-shining gofer for my abuser. I was his 'little boyfriend' and that was all I'd ever be. Nobody would want anything to do with me if they ever found out what was going on. If they knew that my face had been covered in his sperm on countless occasions, that he'd rubbed me over my trousers to get me excited, that I'd been spread-eagle on my single bed, hands and feet bound to the metal frame whilst he humped and grunted away.

And do you know what? I believed him. His words became my 'normal'. Everything he said was true in my mind, and for years following the abuse I lived my life as an invisible, hollow shell. Although I told people of what had happened, built friendships, and had relationships, I never believed for a single second that I was worthy of any kind of decent life. After all, I was soiled, I was worthless, pointless, and thick. Only good as something to be used.

When your every thought is telling you that you're not good enough, you feel that you have no other choice but to believe it. When it's been drilled into you for so long that this is who you are, you can't see past it, and you find yourself looking for things that confirm it. So leaving school with just two 'O' levels proved that he was right. I was 'thick' and would never be anything. But how true was that?

At that point in my life I believed all that I'd been told, and even though the abuse had ended and he was no longer part of my world, his words constantly echoed around my mind. When I was sixteen, I applied to join The Royal Navy. I'm not sure why as the sea scares me. I love looking at it but I find the thought of how deep it is terrifying. On reflection I was just looking for an escape, to get away from where it had all happened but I now realise that it doesn't matter where you go, your head is always with you so unless you can get that straight, there's very little point running. I failed to get into The Royal Navy. No surprise considering that I was 'thick', who did I think I was to consider that I'd be accepted? Why would they want a damaged, worthless, pointless, useless, thicko?

I moved on from that idea and got a job as an apprentice sheet metal worker. Spending my days as a gofer for the welders, I was a dab hand with the sweeping brush, I knew their sandwich orders like the back of my hand, and I had no problem holding the two edges of metal ducting together whilst the welder did his stuff. I didn't even question why they were fully kitted up with protective gloves and masks whilst I was maskless and bare-handed just millimetres from where they were welding. Maybe it was further confirmation that I was worthless? Why would I deserve to be protected?

On the surface these two examples confirmed to me that he was right. I was worthless and thick. Always have been, always will be. But when I look at them from a different angle, another picture begins to emerge. I applied to join the Royal Navy as an Artificer and didn't quite make the grade and was offered the opportunity to take another role. But because I was convinced that I was thick, I didn't even think about it. If I'm honest, as soon as I saw that I hadn't been successful in the role I'd applied for, I dropped into victim mode. Telling myself that it was 'because it was me' and that 'it's all his fault' and 'if it wasn't for what had happened to me I'd have been accepted.' By believing what I'd always been told, I missed out on a career that would have taken me around the world, taught me loads of skills and given me the opportunity to make new friends. My closed mind saw what it wanted to see. It saw a rejection, not an opportunity.

As for the apprenticeship, looking at it through adult eyes, I was treated exactly the same as every other apprentice. It was my job to be the gofer, the lifter, the carrier, and none of us had protective gear. It wasn't because I was worthless, it was just the way it was. But it's only by looking at the situation through different eyes that I see that now. This is all well and good more than 30 years after the event, but the real trick is to be able to see the situations for exactly what they are as they are happening. And to do this we need to constantly challenge our thinking.

If you find yourself in similar situations try asking yourself questions like; 'What evidence do I have to support what I'm thinking? and 'What are the facts here?" Challenge yourself to understand why your thoughts may be defaulting to dis-empowering ones. What is it about the situation that has triggered your automatic negative thoughts and what do you need to concentrate on to transform them into positive, helpful thoughts?

My hope is that the ideas within this book, combined with my lived experiences inspire you to take the steps towards living your life on your terms. As I said earlier, all we have is now, so what better time to start?

"You have trouble living in the present, so you linger in the past because you feel like you never really lived it." Ben Stiller

"You can't run from your memories.
You can't run from the hurt.
You can't run from the constant
feeling that you're not enough.
So you must face it head on."

Steve Nestor

6. Your past does not define you

"Life opens up opportunities to you, and you either take them or you stay afraid of taking them." Jim Carrey

I threw myself down the stairs once. I'm not sure if I've told anybody that before. Funny the things you remember when you write a book. I was about 13 or 14 and couldn't see an end to what was happening to me. When my mum asked what had happened I pretended that I'd fainted at the top of the stairs. There was a boy at school who often fainted in morning assembly (the sickening thud of him hitting the cold wooden floor still sends a chill down my spine now), so I suppose it seemed a feasible reason. I don't think I wanted to die. I don't know why I did it. Attention maybe, or maybe I did want to die. Who knows.

Another time I lay in bed and punched myself in the face a few times. As well as the sexual abuse, he was fond of using me as a punch bag and apart from one time when he hit me in the head and gave me a cauliflower ear he was pretty careful not to leave any visible marks. Kidney punches, jabs to the chest and windings were his go to and I suppose I just wanted somebody to see my black eye and ask me about it so I could tell them what was going on. But nobody did. Nobody noticed. And even if they had asked me about it I'm not sure I'd have told them. I was terrified of him. He was a 'hard man' who was proud of his football violence exploits and the time he'd spent in prison for grievous bodily harm (GBH) and I quickly learned that it was never worth challenging him on anything.

He'd smile and have a laugh with me in front of other people but after he'd been to the Working Men's Club and filled up on lager he'd be dragging me out of bed. Prodding, poking, and punching me for hours, grinding me down, making me feel even more worthless than I already did. He'd ridicule me, ensuring that I 'knew my place' by repeatedly drumming it into me that I was his. His to do with as he pleased, when he pleased. And when he was satisfied that I was completely broken and ready to do what he wanted, he'd make his move. These occasions usually resulted in me being forced to give him a blow job that always took ages due to the fact that he was shit-faced, but occasionally he'd decide that he wanted to get intimate. His rough bristles and Park Drive breath all over my mouth was much worse than anything else he put me through. Give me a beating or violation any day over that level of intimacy. It was in those moments that he'd remind me of our 'special relationship'.

I share these memories simply to show that regardless of what is going on for us at any given moment in our lives, it is exactly that. A moment in time. It is not forever. Bad times will pass and before you know it they are just a memory. As soon as it's done, it's a memory; it's the past, something to learn from and move on from. Please don't confuse 'moving on' with forgetting or doing nothing about it though.

It took me a long time to move on. I wish I'd had the brain I have now when all of this was going on. Hopefully by sharing my experiences I'll be able to help at least one person move on a little quicker than I did. I wasted so many years but there's no point in me regretting that. It's done now and my focus is completely on the here and now and what my future holds.

My past does not define me. The things I went through have certainly shaped me and negatively affected me for a long time but it didn't have to be like that. I didn't seek professional help, maybe that was a mistake, but it didn't feel like an option at the time for some reason. I suppose times were quite different in the Eighties. I'm not sure there was the level of support or understanding that there is now. Esther Rantzen launched Childline[6] in 1986. I was 15 years-old and my years of abuse were coming to an end. I was desperate to leave school, get a job and put everything behind me. What I didn't realise was that it wasn't going to be as easy as that.

Sweeping challenging emotions under the carpet and hoping that it will make itself right definitely wasn't the way to go. And as a coach, it is certainly not something that I'd recommend anybody else to do either. During my late teens and throughout my twenties I drank far too much, got into (if I'm honest, started) a fair few fights, and was, let's just say, not the most faithful partner. Looking back, isn't hindsight a wonderful thing, it's obvious that I saw myself as a victim; somebody who took no responsibility for my actions. It was all somebody else's fault. If my dad hadn't left and if he hadn't done what he did everything would be okay, my life would be perfect.

I know now that I was stuck in a cycle of feeling that I was worthless and that nothing would ever change for me. And do you know what, nothing did change, not in my head anyway. My life wasn't going too bad as it happens but because I was convinced everything would always be bad for me, that's what I focused my attention on. We always see what we want to see and I've learned that the more you look for shit, the more shit you'll find.

"Where focus goes, energy flows." Tony Robbins

I left my job as an apprentice sheet metal worker and went to work for a company building fitted kitchens where I met my best mate, Kenny. But I wasn't settled and wanted to 'escape' so when I was 18 I took a job in the local casino as a trainee croupier with the view to gaining a bit of experience and then travelling the world. It was there that I met my first wife, Jenny. As I mentioned earlier, I feel sorry for the people who knew me back then. They weren't treated the best and I'm not proud of some of the things that I got up to. Needless to say that relationship, through no fault of anybody but me, was always destined to fail. We were together for 12 years, travelled a little, had two wonderful children together (Leah and Dan) and ended up buying a nice semi-detached house. But the negative self-talk constantly reminded me that I wasn't worthy, and I believed it. So I messed up time and again, fuelled by too much beer I regularly got myself into compromising situations.

I know now that all of that time I was denying how I was feeling. I'd convinced myself that I was okay, that I was strong enough to get over what had happened with no help. I didn't want to talk to anybody about it, what help would that be? It's done, let's just leave it alone and move on. But the truth is that I wasn't able to cope with it. I was never diagnosed with any kind of mental illness but for a very long time I felt extremely down, apart from when I was drinking, then I was the complete opposite. All I can say is that I'm glad Facebook wasn't around in those days, it's bad enough knowing that there may be the odd compromising photo of me knocking around somewhere.

I recognise now that I was passively coping with the situation. I felt like there was nothing I could do about it. It was what it was and I had no control over how I felt, my actions and, ultimately, how I made others feel. It was just me.

I know better now and my focus is always on helping other people to decide how they would like to feel and how they would like to move forward. Moving forward could simply be thinking about it from a different perspective, setting a little goal for yourself, talking to a friend or taking the first step towards seeking advice and support from a medical professional, a trained counsellor or therapist (something I am not, and in no way are any of my thoughts, ideas and experiences meant to replace that specialist help that many people need and benefit from).

I take a strengths-based approach to my work, and I truly believe that no matter what we have been through, there are always lessons we can learn from it. Encouraging an active coping attitude is a more helpful way to approach whatever our challenges may be. Rather than burying our head in the sand and hoping for the best, acknowledging that there is something to work through, and focusing on doing something about it is far more empowering. By taking this approach we feel like we're doing something about our challenges and that we have some kind of control over what is happening and how we're feeling. Which of course we do.

The one thing we always have control over is how we respond to the things that are going on around us. As I mentioned earlier, not long after I met Tracy she said "choose to experience it in a different way" when I was sharing how unhappy I was about the things that I'd experienced. I shrugged it off at first, saying something like, 'that's easy for you to say, you didn't go through it.' Looking back, that was me denying that I had any control over how I felt. I was a victim. I had been for as long as I could remember and this type of defensive, dismissive comment was to cause many arguments during the first part of our relationship. I realise now that not only was I not ready to take responsibility for my emotions, I hadn't the first clue how I would go about it. So it was easier to avoid that way of thinking and continue to be a victim, than to put the effort in to change.

We don't always have control of the events that happen to us or those that are happening around us, but we always have a choice of how we'd like to respond; and that response will determine what happens in your future life. I didn't respond in the best way, and for years I was very unhappy; ultimately making those around me unhappy too with my behaviour.

For years I saw the abuse as something that was totally out of my control (which of course it was) but I also believed that my responses were out of my control too. Who wouldn't feel angry, sad, guilty, ashamed, useless, and massively lacking in self-worth in my situation? Surely I was entitled to feel sorry for myself and expect a favour from the world after what I'd been through. But it doesn't work like that. I realise that now. There is only one person who controls how you feel… and that person is you. Regardless of what anybody says and does, you always have the power to decide how you'd like to respond.

I used to live my life waiting for somebody to make me feel better but even when things were going okay, it didn't make much of a difference. I constantly had a knot in my stomach reminding me of how useless I was and how I didn't deserve anything other than being used. I felt invisible. It was as if I didn't really exist so when I was noticed by somebody – let's say I was out in a club and a woman smiled at me, I'd be so flattered that I'd been 'seen' that I'd quickly end up in a compromising situation.

Apparently, promiscuity is common in people who have been sexually abused (it's a good job I didn't know that at the time as it would have given me another excuse to not take responsibility for my actions). One theory suggests that by taking numerous sexual partners, the abused are looking to put as much space between themselves and their abusers as possible. Others talk of the abuse being so normalised that its lasting effects are that the abused feel that they have to be sexually desirable to have any self-worth. I can relate to both of these ideas. But the 'good' feelings never lasted very long. Most of the encounters I had were one-night stands. We're talking about the days before mobile phones and social media so I only saw these people after a few too many drinks, often without exchanging full names, and invariably the encounters were instantly forgettable (and undoubtedly regrettable) for both parties.

Sex has always been a challenging issue for me and has got me into 'trouble' on more than one occasion. Even in the early years of my relationship with Tracy, I still associated sex with being liked. If Tracy didn't want sex with me I'd convince myself that she didn't like me and that it was only a matter of time before the relationship would end. I was never unfaithful to Tracy but in these moments it was common for me to be moody and pick an argument. Luckily she could see 'me', she has been able to since the moment we met. That's not to say we didn't argue, we had some real 'humdingers' but in time I realised that that was okay. It didn't mean that she was going to leave me, or that she didn't like me. I'd just pissed her off with my moods.

And there lies the point. It was always me that was the problem. I'd never tackled my underlying issues, I'd convinced myself that I was okay, that as I was getting older everything was working itself out. What a load of rubbish that was. The story of my life (as I believed it) was fuelling my behaviour. I believed that I was useless. I believed that to be liked I had to be wanted sexually. I believed that nobody could ever love me. And these beliefs manifested themselves time and again in the things I was saying and in the ways I was acting. But how accurate were they? I know now that this was my abuser's story that he wanted me to believe. It made it easier for him to control me, to take what he wanted from me, to make me feel grateful for the attention that he gave me. For years after the abuse ended I believed this story and I told it to myself endlessly. My negative self-thoughts were all consuming so that even when I was shown genuine friendship and love I couldn't see it. There's a great quote by the author Kemi Sogunle that sums this up perfectly:

"Be mindful of your thoughts. Your thoughts become your words. Your words become your actions. Your actions become your reality."

If I'm honest I still feel this way at times if I allow myself to. The scars from the damage that was done all those years ago are still there, and the wounds have never completely healed. But I'm okay with that now because I know that I have control of when I let those feelings in. It's natural to feel a huge range of emotions and to not recognise that the things that we've experienced can never be completely swept away can be as damaging as not attempting to deal with them in the first place. Sometimes we must sit with the reality of how we're feeling, regardless of how uncomfortable that is, as this allows us to understand what's going on for us, what the triggers are, and how we really feel. Brushing our emotions under the carpet is not helpful for anyone.

When I was a support worker I remember manning a stall at a networking event and striking up a conversation with the people next to me who offered mental health support in the community. I didn't share my story with them, but somehow we got onto the subject of childhood sexual abuse with one of them sharing the experience of a man in his sixties who had recently been to them for help (without breaching any confidentiality obviously). This gentleman had apparently lived a very successful life. He had a lovely family, lots of friends, and had built a lucrative business for himself, but recently he had been struggling with his mental health. He was sexually abused as a boy but had never shared his story with anybody. He'd buried it deep within himself, denying that it had even happened. His family, friends, and business associates had no idea of what he had been through so when he started struggling to cope and experiencing anxiety and deep depression nobody could understand what was happening. To the outside world, he had the perfect life.

During their conversations he admitted that it all began to unravel as he reached a point in his life where he was considering selling his business and retiring. All of a sudden, his past caught up with him and 'hit him like a train.' And in the subsequent conversations he'd begun to realise that his drive for the 'perfect' life had been fuelled by his abuse, and that he'd never appreciated what he had as he was so focussed on moving foward and achieving the next goal that he'd set for himself.

Hearing this made me stop and think about where I was and how I wanted to feel. My progress has been a slow burner, and little things have influenced and inspired me along the way, this conversation being just one of them. I can totally relate to the 'moving forward' thing. Although I've recently realised that a more accurate description of this for me would be 'running away from.' I was always a 'grass is greener on the other side of the fence' type of person. Whatever I was doing I was always thinking about what the next thing is. Whenever we went on holiday, instead of enjoying where we were I wouldn't allow myself to relax, I'd be busy seeking out somewhere new to explore. Whatever job I was doing, I would tell myself that I needed to move on to be happy. This pattern was replicated throughout all of my behaviours. I was never settled or content. I went through life thinking that this was just how I was and there was nothing I could do about it. I'd always thought that when the children grew up and left home, we'd sell up and live abroad or by the sea in the UK. I loved the idea of living in a different city for six months at a time and experiencing life as the locals would. Life is too short to stay in one place and do one thing. As they say, variety is the spice of life. I realise now that I was always dreaming of running away but regardless of where I went and what I did, I would always be me. Worthless, useless, thick, me.

During the Covid-19 Pandemic we became really good friends with our neighbours Rob and Kelly. Sparked by a VE Day (socially-distanced) street party we began to get to know one another better. When we were allowed to meet in gardens, we took the opportunity to share some food and a few drinks with them. And it was during that evening that I realised something fundamental about myself.

I've spent my life running away and looking for the next thing rather than appreciating what I have right in front of me. We were talking about possibly living by the sea and I was simply asked 'why do you think that would make you happy?' I couldn't give any other answer apart from that it was something that I'd always thought I'd need to do to be happy. It sounds like nothing now I've written it down, but that moment, and the many self-reflection moments that followed it, helped me realise how happy, settled and content I am in my life; I just hadn't taken the time to notice as I was too concerned with thinking about the next thing and trying to live up to the story that I'd been telling myself my whole life.

We live by the stories we tell ourselves and I had told myself that I needed to move to the seaside to be happy. But how old was that story? On reflection, it dates back to when I was a child growing up in that abusive household in the Midlands where my happiest memories were of spending time with my grandparents and the odd trip to the seaside. I went to Paignton in Devon once with them but it was usually just a day trip to Rhyl or Blackpool that was organised by the local working men's club committee. For the coach journey we got a carton of juice and a bag of crisps, and a little bit of pocket money in a paper bag to spend on whatever we wanted. In those moments I remember being truly happy.

We're constantly growing and changing but our thoughts and beliefs are sometimes left behind, creating a danger that we are held back from living a life on our terms, true to the very moment that we are in. It's so important to constantly question your thoughts and beliefs, and I'll be forever grateful to Rob and Kelly for helping me to question mine which enabled me to break free from them. It's thanks to that conversation that I've realised I've no longer got to run away from anything. I can relax and enjoy my life.

This isn't to say that I'm settling for what I have. I still like the idea of experiencing life as a local in different cities and the seaside still has a certain pull for me. I have hopes, dreams and aspirations to make my life even better than it is today. But the difference between the me of a few years ago and the me of 2023 is that I'm no longer running away from anything. I've worked hard to build a strong base from which to grow and I'm fundamentally happy and just need a few tweaks here and there to bring more joy to my life.

I mentioned a recent trip to Fuerteventura at the beginning of this book and that week in the sun in January 2023 was a reminder of just how important it is for me to be true to myself and to do everything I can to live a life on my terms. Watching the sunrise over the Atlantic Ocean every morning, looking up at the wispy clouds whilst relaxing in the heat, enjoying a beer at La Isla Chiringuito bar whilst eavesdropping on the waves crashing against the black volcanic rocks, listening to the audiobook version of Somebody I Used to Know by Wendy Mitchell[7], (a powerful reminder of how precious life is and how important it is to live in the moment), chatting with the lovely Rosanna from the animation team who shared her passion for all things Korean, singing, and making people smile, all contributed to me formulating a plan for the next stage of my life.

If I'm honest with myself, I didn't want to go home. I could easily have stayed in the Canary Islands and on our final morning both my wife and I were feeling a little low (I actually wrote these few lines on Saturday morning on my sunbed after our conversation). We talked about not looking forward to going home to the cold, wet weather. Although I enjoy my job, the thought of work on Monday morning didn't fill me with joy. The state of politics in the UK was also a contributing factor in us not wanting to head home too. Workers striking, the NHS on its knees, the economy struggling, and fuel costs crippling many households. All of these things seem a million miles away and totally unimportant when you watch the sunrise over the ocean and, in the big scheme of things, they are.

We had a little moan but our attention quickly turned to thinking about what we can control and the steps we could take, if we chose to. We talked about how, if we wanted to, we could change our lives tomorrow. Our youngest son is 18 this year and the only commitment we'll have then is our gorgeous Cockapoo, Obi who we could make the arrangements for to ensure that we could take him with us if we decided to make a change and move to sunnier climes. We discussed how we could, if we chose to, work from anywhere in the world doing the work that we do. In a post-Covid world where virtual working is the norm for many (including us), as long as we have a laptop and an internet connection we can work and earn money. That's assuming we decided to carry on doing what we're doing. After all, it's a big world out there with endless possibilities; who knows what passions and interests await us. As I write this I'm not sure what changes (if any) we'll make, or whether we'll decide to take the plunge and live abroad at some point in our lives, but the important thing here is that we have realised that we have options. If things aren't bringing us as much joy as we want in our lives, we have the power to do something about it. Whatever happens, this week in the winter sun has taught me even more about myself and has confirmed that I'm not ready to settle just yet. Watch this space.

Please don't make the same mistakes as the younger me. Take responsibility for yourself, for your emotions, for your present self and for your future self. And the sooner the better, believe me, you'll thank yourself for it. "Choose to experience it in a different way" underpins all that is good in my life and is my 'go to' whenever something happens to me or around me. Try this to see how it might work for you too…

Think of something that you've been through (or are currently going through) that is bothering you, causing you unhappiness, stress or making you feel anxious. Write it down at the top of a piece of paper and create two lists beneath it. Firstly list all of the things you've thought about and the actions you've taken with regards to it and make a note of where you are and how you're feeling. Now make a second list. This time write down some alternatives to what you've already done. The trick here is to open your mind and to take away all of your usual constraints and see things from a different angle. 'Remove' yourself from the situation, pretend you're watching yourself and the situation unfold on the TV. Take a 'helicopter view' and pull back from the detail to see the bigger picture and to get more perspective and a different view of what's going on.

Very often we're far too close to what's happening to be able to think differently and it's easy for our minds to become closed off. And when this happens we can start to believe that where we are and how we feel is where we'll always be. And the more we think like that, the more likely it is that we will be 'stuck' so we need to be able to see alternatives, to realise that we do have choices and that very often we are the ones getting in our own way. There are many things that we have no control over, but we always have the power to decide how we'd like to feel. And we always have the power to change the way we look at and think about things.

I'm not saying that this stuff is easy. It takes practice and a commitment from you that you really want things to change. But if you do, you have complete control over making it happen. If you're struggling to see an alternative, a useful tip is to ask yourself what others might think and do in your situation. For example, what would the following say;

- Your best friend or favourite family member
- A total stranger
- An alien from outer space
- Your favourite singer/actor/sports star
- Your favourite cartoon character or superhero

- The person you respect most in the world
- Your least favourite person (real or fictional)
- You. Five years ago, and in five years-time.

Now that you've begun to explore what other options may be available to you, what will you do differently? And how might taking that alternative approach affect the outcome and the way you're feeling?

"If you change the way you look at things, the things you look at change." Wayne Dyer

7. I'm a survivor (no I'm not)

"Here is a test to find whether your mission on earth is finished: If you're alive it isn't." Richard Bach

The Oxford Dictionary (online)[8] definition of survivor is:

A person who continues to live, especially despite being nearly killed or experiencing great danger or difficulty;

- the sole/only survivor of the massacre
- The plane crashed in an area of dense jungle. There were no survivors.

I'm not a big fan of labels. I saw something once that said 'Labels are for soup cans, not humans' and I quite like that. They feel like an easy way for others to describe you for their records. It seems to me that if you've been abused (regardless of the type of abuse you've endured) and have 'come through it' you are given some kind of pat on the back and then placed into the neat little 'survivors' box.

I'm not entirely sure where I'm going with this so just stay with me while I work through it; hopefully it will make sense soon. The term 'survivor' might be okay for some people who have been abused; it's not for me to say what others are and are not bothered by, but something about it just doesn't sit right with me. I feel like it implies that I shouldn't have gotten through what I did. That my life should have ended because of those things that happened to me. The more I think about it (I usually talk to think, in this case I'm writing to think), the more I begin to understand why I don't like the term.

During the six years or so that I was physically, sexually, and psychologically abused I was made to feel 'lucky' that somebody would want anything to do with me. I was made to feel grateful that I was allowed to be part of his life, I was even made to feel thankful when I didn't receive a beating. So to be classed as a survivor, and all the implications that (in my mind) come with that, just seems to reinforce the messages that he buried deep in my psyche; that I am worthless and useless; with an added twist of 'what are you still doing here' for good measure.

For a long time I've passively accepted that I don't like 'survivor' and have got internally annoyed whenever I've heard the term being used. It wasn't until a conversation that I was having with a friend of mine, the inspirational Aimee Bateman, that I really started to consider the impact that the use of the word had been having on me all of these years. And what you're witnessing as you read these few lines is me working through this challenge in real time. Who knows where it will go!

It's tough thinking things through, unpicking all of the thoughts that have been your 'normal' and questioning what they mean, where they come from, and what truth is within them. Who would have thought that more than 35 years after my abuse ended that I'd be sitting in front of my laptop mulling over and examining the impact that one single word has had on me all of this time.

You might think that a word is the least of your problems when you've been abused, and you may be right. The reality is, the abuse ended a long time ago but the control that was embedded during that time lingers. Language is one of the most powerful forms of control that humans have over each other so regardless of whether the words came from his mouth or not, the implications, the triggers, and the control is always there. Holding me down, putting me back in my place, reminding me that I am worthless, useless, and 'lucky' to be here. And as such I should be grateful to be allowed simply to breathe (and not get a daily beating). Why should I expect any more from life if my childhood experiences should have resulted in my death?

That went a bit deeper than I expected but that's what happens when we create the time to reflect and to be truly honest with ourselves. By unpicking things that we have always accepted we can begin to really understand ourselves. And once we can do this we can start to knock down the barriers that may have been getting in our way, and replace them with open roads that can lead us to wherever we choose to go.

The impact of the word 'survivor' will always control me. If I allow it to. There are some things that we just can't control. And I can't control whether people want to class me as a survivor or not. I can't control what others write, think, or say. I can't change what he said to me. I can't change what happened when I was a child, and I can't change my past thoughts and behaviours. But what I can do is to decide how I want to feel now and how I want to feel in the future. As I've said a few times already (and I don't apologise for repeating this as it's an important message to understand and practice), we don't always have control over what happens, but we always have the power to decide how we'd like to respond to it.

Realising how you don't want to feel is the first important step to understanding what you do want; and once you've uncovered that, you can start to work towards it. And there lies the key; work towards. Very often we decide what we don't want and we focus our attention there. But where we focus our attention is where our energy goes.

For example, for years I'd been about three stone overweight and every so often I looked in the mirror and thought things like; "I don't want my belly to overhang my trousers." and more recently, "I don't want to be fat and 50." Big mistake. My focus was always on what I didn't want, not what I did want. So a couple of years ago I turned my attention to deciding what I wanted and set my goals accordingly.

I wanted to be 14 stone and I wanted to feel fitter, healthier, and stronger. And six months later, just in time for my 50th birthday, I was. My focus helped me to decide how I was going to get to where I wanted to be (I walk at least 10,000 steps a day, use my kettlebells at least four times a week, and I watch my calorie intake). I set mini-goals along the way (e.g. lose one pound a week) and decided to not get downhearted and give up if I didn't lose any weight in a particular week or if I had a 'bad' day. It's all about the long-term plan; losing the weight and keeping it off.

And I'm doing this by focusing on what I want and how I want to feel. By setting a goal and working towards something positive and not away from negativity. In giving ourselves the best chance of flourishing in life, it's crucial that instead of working away from something (e.g. I don't want to be overweight, I don't want to work here anymore, I don't want to feel this way, I don't want to be in this relationship etc.) we turn our attention to where we do want to be and how we do want to feel… and then begin to take the actions that will help us to get there.

And it feels appropriate here to mention the power of 'yet'. How often do we say we can't do something, or are not good at something? For example, I've always said that I can't play a musical instrument. I briefly tried to play the trumpet when I was at primary school, and I had a quick go on my son's guitar once before reminding myself that I'm not musical, and can't play an instrument. But recently I've decided to give playing the banjo a go; and it's all thanks to the power of 'yet.'

Let me explain. It's easy to say things like; 'I'm no good at… I don't understand… I can't do it…' and just leave it there, believing that we are stuck and unable to learn new things, gain new skills, feel more positive emotions, and move forward. But by simply adding the word 'yet' to the end of our sentence we change our language and thoughts from negativity, to possibility. And that's the key word here, 'possibility.' I'm not saying that adding the word 'yet' will make everything okay, and that you will definitely be able to do that thing; but it will open your mind and give you hope that you may be able to.

Taking my banjo playing as an example, I could easily have stuck with 'I can't play the banjo', but by adding 'yet' and expanding my thinking I ended up with a different thought process. I can't play the banjo…yet. But if I bought or borrowed one, watched some YouTube videos, read some books, took some lessons, practised regularly… I might just be able to learn.

It's slow-going with my banjo playing but I've learned how to tune it. I've learned a few chords and have been practising my strumming and finger-picking techniques and I set myself a goal of being able to play a tune on it by the time I was 51. And I'm pleased to say that I learned the Bonnie Banks of Loch Lomond in time for my birthday. I won't win any awards for my banjo playing but I've proved to myself (again) that if I open my mind, set goals, put in the time and believe in myself I can achieve pretty much whatever I set out to do. Which brings me to the publication of this book.

Writing it was one challenge but I have written quite a lot over the years (blogs, articles for websites, reports, Open University essays) so I was fairly confident that I could get the words down on paper. But when it came to editing and publishing, well that was a different story. This is the first book I've ever written so I didn't have a clue where to start. Luckily, through my LinkedIn connections which I've worked hard to grow and build relationships with, I know a couple of experts in the field. Leila and Ali are brother and sister and own Known Publishing and they recently helped a friend of mine, the very talented Tim Roberts publish his first book, Break the Mould. So who better to chat with than them about the process of getting my book published and on the shelves of 'all good book stores'.

I booked in a call with Ali and he explained the process, from editing, design, proofreading, and typesetting all the way through to getting it ready as an Ebook, paperback, and hardback and then onto marketing. It was a great conversation and gave me loads of food for thought, as have all of my chats with Leila and Ali. As I said, I've never written a book before and I was under the impression that you need a publisher to be seen as a credible author so, over the weekend I thought about the services that they offer, but the more I thought about it, the more I realised that going down the 'publisher' route just wasn't for me. So I started trawling through the internet looking into other options. I've always liked a challenge and just because I've never published a book before, it didn't mean that I could never do it. I haven't published a book… yet. But with some research, a lot of determination, and a desire to show that, given the opportunity, I can turn my hand to most things, I was sure that I'd be able to work it out.

I learnt about ISBNs and Imprint names, and found myself down more than one rabbit hole in my quest to discover my best options for publishing. I had to remind myself why this book is so important to me. It's not about getting to the top of the best-seller list, making money from it, or positioning myself a 'thought-leader' in order to get more work and grow my business (which is good as I don't own a business). The reason I've written it is to give hope wherever it may be needed and I just wanted to get it out there for anybody who might benefit from my reflections. This thinking led me to decide that self-publishing with Amazon via KDP (Kindle Direct Publishing) was the way to go.

One the aims of this book is to show that you don't have to have money or be famous to have your voice heard. We're all as important as each other and we all have a story to tell so it didn't feel right to me to use a publisher when I can self-publish for a relatively small amount (as could you if you chose to). My friends and family have helped me with the editing process. Their feedback on the content, suggestions on the grammar, spotting typos and repetition have all been invaluable in getting this book published and I'll be forever grateful to each and every one of them for taking the time to help me out. When I decided to self-publish I had no idea what I was getting in to but here it is, my debut book has made it into the world and will forever be something that I'm immensely proud of.

Expanding our thinking helps us to feel that there are other possibilities out there. That we're not stuck, that we can learn new things, make new friends, get that promotion, write that book, play that instrument, get that qualification, and feel 'happier' than we do at the moment. Once we change our thoughts and language from negativity, to that of possibility our lives become richer and we begin to see opportunities rather than dead-ends.

What can't you do… yet?

"The first step to getting the things you want out of life is this: Decide what you want." Ben Stein

8. Life is ACE (or is it?)

"The Old West is not a certain place in a certain time, it's a state of mind. It's whatever you want it to be." Tom Mix

I love the word 'ace'. When people ask me how I am, if I'm feeling good I'll very often say that I'm ace. For many it simply means excellent, or really good - but for others it has a very different meaning.

ACE stands for Adverse Childhood Experiences. I'm not sure when the terminology was first used but it certainly wasn't in my vocabulary when I was growing up. According to Young Minds[9], Adverse Childhood Experiences (ACEs) are "highly stressful, and potentially traumatic, events or situations that occur during childhood and/or adolescence. They can be a single event, or prolonged threats to, and breaches of, the young person's safety, security, trust or bodily integrity."

The NHS[10] gives some examples of ACEs as being:

- Physical abuse (tick)
- Sexual Abuse (tick)
- Emotional Abuse (tick)

- Living with someone who abused drugs (possible tick)
- Living with someone who abused alcohol (tick)
- Exposure to domestic violence (tick)
- Living with someone who has gone to prison (tick)
- Living with someone with serious mental illness (probable tick)
- Losing a parent through divorce, death, or abandonment (tick).

The NHS also share that in a 2014 UK study on ACEs, 47% of people experienced at least one ACE with 9% of the population having 4+ ACEs. I'm not sure what percentage have 7 ACEs to their name but that's how my stats read. And looking at that in black and white, I could feel quite sorry for myself. Something I did for a very long time.

Long before I'd heard of ACEs I knew that I'd lived through some terrible experiences, but at the time it was just my life. I had no control over it, it was happening to me, and going on around me. Starting with my dad, although I don't remember him being around much, I knew that he'd hit my mum and that he was an alcoholic. And when he left and was replaced with him, my ACEs increased. As you can see from the tick list above, I've almost got a full house. I'm not sure that he ever used drugs, I think I remember hearing cannabis mentioned once or twice but it's not something I can definitely 'tick', and I would argue that he almost certainly lived with a serious mental illness but, to my knowledge was never diagnosed, so I'll leave that off my list too as I think seven is enough to be going on with.

According to the NHS, 'the longer an individual experiences an ACE and the more ACEs someone experiences, the bigger the impact it will have on their development and their health'… with some impacts of ACEs including;

- An increase in the risk of certain health problems in adulthood, such as cancer and heart disease, as well as increasing the risk of mental health difficulties, violence and becoming a victim of violence
- An increase in the risk of mental health problems, such as anxiety, depression, and post-traumatic stress. 1 in 3 diagnosed mental health conditions in adulthood directly relate to ACEs
- The ability to recognise and manage different emotions.
- The capacity to make and keep healthy friendships and other relationships
- The ability to manage behaviour in school settings.
- Difficulties coping with emotions safely without causing harm to self or others.

I'm quite glad in a way that I didn't know all that stuff and had never heard of ACEs when I was younger. Somehow I feel like it would have given me even more of an excuse to have acted like a victim, something I didn't need as I was doing a pretty good job without the label. I understand that it's important to recognise these things, to give things names and labels so that more people gain a greater understanding of how these factors affect people in adulthood and I'm not for one minute saying that we shouldn't have these frameworks. But for me, having a label like this might have given me a licence to never take responsibility for myself as an adult.

Even as I write this, more than 35 years after my abuse ended, I could easily drop into victim mode again. How unfair was it that I was exposed to all of those things? How different might my life had been if I'd had a 'normal' childhood? What decisions might I have made if I'd had loving, caring, nurturing parents? But you know what. It doesn't matter anymore. It's now that counts. As I said earlier, all I have is now and spending my life thinking about the 'what ifs' is going to do me no favours whatsoever. That's not to say that I never think about my past, of course I do. But I do it from a different perspective than when I was younger.

The 'Reflect' aspect to my 'Reflect, Believe, Grow' framework is all about looking back on situations that you've encountered and taking the lessons from them. For example, when something goes well, how do you ensure that you take the time to celebrate the wins, to practise gratitude, to recognise all that's good in our lives, and to build on what's gone well to get even better.

We can do something similar when we look back on the things that haven't gone so well in our lives. What lessons have we learned from our mistakes, and what do we know about ourselves when we reflect on what we've been through? For example, when I think of my experiences I realise that, if nothing else, I'm resilient… especially when you consider some of the impact that the NHS link with ACEs. By recognising this about myself, I can use it as a foundation to build from. When we understand that we're not broken and that we have strengths despite the things we've been through, we can start to believe that we are more than our experiences. And this is crucial in moving forward and living a life on our terms.

As I mentioned earlier, we can often feel stuck in time, believing that nothing will change, that things will always be 'this way.' By reflecting on our experiences, and taking the positives from them, we can start to see that things can (and do) change.

And we are the catalyst for that change. We are the ones who control how we feel, we are the ones who decide what is right for us, we are the ones who can take the actions that will help us to get to where we want to be. Us, and us alone, have the power within ourselves to live the kind of life that is right for us. If we only believe it.

I nearly didn't write this book. I started and stopped so many times; questioning who would be interested in what I had to say. But every time I doubted myself something happened that reminded me why I had this idea in the first place and why it is so important to me. I'd share a little of my experience with somebody and they'd say how much it helped, I'd talk about what my purpose is and how finding it has helped me, and others have said what a difference I've made to them. And a couple of times when I've doubted myself, this quote has appeared on my social media feeds, giving me the motivation I needed to share my story;

"One day you will tell your story of how you've overcome what you are going through now, and it will become part of someone else's survival guide."

You can't run from the hurt

There's a lot of talk around about how important finding your purpose and meaning in life is, and I can't emphasise enough what a difference this has made to me in all aspects of my life. I've talked about how my purpose is to stimulate reflection, inspire belief, and to ignite growth and I try to keep this in mind in everything that I do. Whether it's keeping in check the way I talk to myself, the interactions I have with others, starting a new project, staying on track towards the goals I've set for myself, or reminding the people around me of what they're hoping to achieve.

In times of doubt it's been invaluable to have this purpose ingrained into my thinking. Knowing what I'm all about and why the things I do are so important to me only serves to enable and empower me to carry on towards my goals. For example, knowing that the reason I've written this book is to not only give hope, support and direction to anyone who needs it, but to fulfil part of my own personal mission.

I've come to realise that for me life isn't about getting to the next place or milestone. I spent years believing that I would be happy when… my abuser left, when I left home, when I worked abroad, when I bought a house, when I got a better job, when I was my own boss… the list goes on. Really, all I was doing during those years was wishing my life away. I didn't take the time to step back and enjoy what was good in my life. I was too busy trying to run away.

But regardless of how far you run, you've always got your brain with you. You can't run from your memories. You can't run from the hurt. You can't run from the constant feeling that you're not enough. You can't run from the words in your head telling you that you are useless, thick, and worthless.

I learned that there was no point running. I needed to face all that crap head on. But to do so I had to build my resilience. I had to dig deep and reflect on all that had gone before. I've mentioned that I believe that regardless of the circumstance we find ourselves in there is always something to learn. And one of my biggest learnings when I look back on the years that I was living through sexual, psychological, and physical abuse at the hands of my mum's boyfriend is the fact that it wasn't all bad.

That might sound strange, but the reality is that I wasn't being abused, beaten, or bullied for every single second of every single day during those six years of my life. But for years following the abuse, that's all I thought about. My focus and attention were on the bad things that happened; not surprisingly as there were plenty of horrendous experiences that I went through. I know

now that that kind of thinking didn't help me at all; but at the time it felt impossible to shake. I believed that I would always feel that way. And why shouldn't I? In my mind every aspect of my life was tainted by the way I was treated by him.

Whenever I thought about my childhood my mind always went to the bad stuff. But for every bad thing I experienced, there was at least one good thing to balance it out. I just never took the time to see it that way. But by realising that part of my purpose is to stimulate reflection (in myself and others) I started to look back at things and see them from a different angle.

For example, I have a clear memory of coming home later than I was told to one day and taking a proper beating for it. I was prodded in the chest and punched in the stomach. I was sent to my room and made to lie face-down on the bed and wait with my jeans and pants around my ankles, my bare bottom exposed. I was left there for what seemed like hours until the door creaked open and I was beaten again with a leather belt. I still remember the searing pain as the metal buckle whipped against my skin.

But when I look beyond that beating, I had a good day that day. I'd been a typical young boy spending time with some friends playing football on the school field before moving on to the woods close to where we lived. We'd played on a rope swing, swinging as high as we could before dropping into the soft ferns and pretending to be soldiers hiding in the undergrowth. I remember having such a good time that I put my watch back an hour (these were the days before Smart watches). I thought that was a clever move at the time, but I realised how wrong I was when I found myself doubled up on the floor later that evening following his punch to my guts.

When I look back now I don't focus on the fear and pain I felt when I got home. I focus on the extra hour of fun that I had, the feeling of happiness and freedom, the liberating experience of losing myself and escaping to a make-believe world where we were a platoon of soldiers on a secret mission. And the lessons I've taken from it all.

As I've said throughout this book, life is just a series of moments to experience, to enjoy whenever possible, and to learn from. And apart from the obvious lesson of not lying and putting my watch back an hour, when I think about it, that experience (and many, many similar ones) have taught me to enjoy the good times. To look out for the things that make your heart sing. To recognise when you are smiling. To take note of when you lose yourself. To embrace all the good that life has to offer. To breathe those moments in and hold them in your mind to refer to when things are not going so well. Because, let's face it, things don't go well all of the time but by reminding ourselves of the good stuff, we can begin to get a more balanced view of how our world really is.

I'm not talking here about pushing the bad memories or thoughts out of your mind, because by doing that there's a chance that they'll come back and hit you like a train one day. This is simply about taking a step back and looking at the situation in a more holistic way. Acknowledge the way that you feel, make note of all the crap, but don't allow it to take over because, in my experience, that's only going to lead to a lifetime of hurt. Hurt that only you feel. I've realised that the person who abused me wasn't feeling my pain when I was no longer in his life (or even when I was for that matter). But for years I was carrying it around. Constantly reminding myself how bad my childhood was. How it wasn't fair that it had happened to me. That if it wasn't for him I would have been successful and happy.

Don't get me wrong, I don't knock myself for the impact his actions had on me and I recognise that the years of abuse will have a lasting effect on me for the rest of my life. But reflecting on the past 35 years or so since he was in my life, I definitely could have taken control of my emotions much sooner than I did. If I'd only understood how possible it was to become unstuck. If I'd known that the power to feel positive, resilient, and confident lay in my hands all along I would have taken the steps I have much sooner.

Having said that, I do truly believe that everything I have experienced has been for a reason and I am exactly where I should be at this moment in time. Maybe I was meant to experience everything I've been through? In an ideal world these kinds of things wouldn't happen to anybody, anywhere, ever. But there are plenty of us out there who will tell you that we don't live in an ideal world and without it happening to me I wouldn't be sitting here on a Saturday morning sharing my reflections and offering hope and support to anyone who may need it at this moment in time.

"ONCE WE CHANGE OUR THOUGHTS AND LANGUAGE FROM NEGATIVITY, TO THAT OF POSSIBILITY OUR LIVES BECOME RICHER AND WE BEGIN TO SEE OPPORTUNITIES RATHER THAN DEAD-ENDS."

STEVE NESTOR

9. I still feel sad at times

"I love walking in the rain because no one can see me crying." Rowan Atkinson

If I allowed myself to, I could easily drop into 'victim' mode and spend my days feeling sorry for myself. But what good would that do? It's often the smallest things that might trigger an unhappy memory. The abuse wasn't just sexual, as well as the physical abuse where I was regularly treated like a human punchbag, there was the more subtle, psychological abuse that was a constant in my life.

I was the skivvy, the gofer, the job doer, the tea-maker, the cleaner and the shopper. Now that's probably the 'norm' for many people, helping out and doing chores around the house is commonplace in most families. But do most children have to sit with their hands in the freezing cold water of the toilet, scraping off limescale with an old kitchen knife until every last speck was chipped away from the enamel. I'm not sure what was happening in our house, but that toilet seemed to be a breeding ground for limescale. It feels like every other week I was leaning over the bowl, scraping away, always with the threat of a kidney punch (or worse) hanging over me if I didn't get it spotless.

Do most families make their children wash every single pot, pan, bowl, plate, baking tray, tin, cup, glass, saucer, and piece of cutlery in the house if they leave the slightest mark on any of the dishes they wash up that day? Do most children have to run a bath for the man who only minutes earlier was humping away on top of them? And whilst he's in the bath, do most children have to iron his jeans, ensuring there is the sharpest crease possible running down the centre of them, and polish his black shoes so that you can 'see your face' in them? Do most children have to deliver a lit cigarette to their abuser whilst he's lying in the bath that you've filled for him? Do most children have to stand outside a bookmakers with a list of bets to place for their abuser, waiting for someone willing to take it inside and place it for them, absolutely terrified with every minute that passes that the bets won't be placed in time and the consequences that they'll face when they get home if that's the case? I hope not.

Because what I experienced wasn't about helping out, pulling my weight, or earning my pocket money. It was another way of him controlling me. Another way of him keeping me in my place, of making me feel that my role in life was to serve him; to do whatever he wanted, whenever he wanted me to do it. And it's these small things that can stick with me. I'll (hopefully) never be forced into a sexual act again and I'll never be a scared child again worried about getting a beating. But I do have to do the dishes, iron my clothes and clean the house, and if I'm not careful those everyday chores could easily tip me into a spiral of negative thoughts.

Luckily I've been able to share all of my experiences, thoughts and fears with Tracy and whenever I have a moment I'm able to talk about it, nip it in the bud and put it into perspective. But it hasn't always been that way. For years those 'little' triggers caused me so much grief. My mind would wander back to my childhood and before I knew it I felt like I was sitting within a big black cloud. Not able to see anything but darkness all around me. I couldn't feel any hope for the future, I remember thinking that I would always be tied to my past. And the more I thought about it, the stronger became the 'reality' that my life was, and always would be, pointless!

It was in these moments that I felt real sadness, sadness that occasionally still creeps up on me now. Sadness that my mum wasn't there to protect me from the abuse I was suffering. Even when she found out she did nothing about it. And since it's all ended she's never apologised or tried to make amends in any way. She sends birthday and Christmas cards and even includes a bit of cash but it means nothing. I wanted her to be there when I was at my most vulnerable, but she was nowhere to be seen. Maybe she was scared of him, which is completely understandable as I know he used to beat her too, but that doesn't excuse the lack of care shown to her child then and since.

Sadness that I never had a dad. Although my mum and dad didn't split up until I was about eight years-old, I don't remember him being around much. He was in the navy and then worked on the oil rigs so spent a lot of time away from home apparently, and even when he was there I have no memories of ever doing anything with him. I didn't know him at all and between the ages of eight and eighteen he disappeared completely from my life. It turns out he'd made his way (somehow) to Australia and had been living in North Bundaberg. Completely out of the blue, he appeared on my doorstep when I was about 23. And after the initial shock wore off, it soon became clear that he wasn't interested in me or anything to do with my life; he was more interested in the local cannabis dealer and it wasn't long before he disappeared again. The next thing I heard was that he'd died of a massive heart attack at the age of 51 back in Australia.

The fact that he was 51 when he died has been playing on mind quite a bit over the last couple of years. As I write this, I am 51 years-old and my aim is to get this book published as close to my 52nd birthday (May 2023) as possible. I've made great progress in my life since realising that I have control over how I want to feel, but I'm becoming increasingly aware of my mortality. Getting to 52 years of age will release me from the fear that I'll die at the same age as my dad. When I think about it rationally there's no reason why I won't reach 52.

My dad was an alcoholic and a drug user, he smoked and lived an unhealthy lifestyle by all accounts, I heard that he had spent time living on the streets. I'm not Mr Fitness by any means and I love a drink with friends, and enjoy a nice whisky at the end of the night but I've never smoked or taken drugs (unless you count Poppers and half a cigar in Cuba) and although I do enjoy the odd Doner kebab and bag of chips, I think I've got a relatively balanced diet. I have a good job, a lovely home, an amazing wife and fabulous children. But being rational isn't always that easy and these are the times that I have to focus my attention to ensure that I'm seeing the world for how it actually is, and not just peeking at a sliver of it through a gap in the curtains. We all have our very own window on the world, but to ensure that we live a life completely on our terms we need to open that view up. We need to see the world from all angles. We need to take a wider view that will enable us to see the whole picture. A view that will let us take everything into consideration; to see the reality of the situation, and not just our blinkered view of what we think the situation is.

Over the years I've told myself that it doesn't bother me that I don't have a dad, or a mum that cares. I've told myself the stories that I want to hear. Because convincing myself that I'm not bothered makes it easier to avoid the reality that I am actually really sad about it. Because I knew there was nothing that I could do to change the situation, I thought that the only way to deal with it was to detach and protect myself by telling myself that I didn't care, even convincing myself that it was better not to have loving parents.

I realise now that this way of dealing with things isn't healthy. I've only been lying to myself all these years and although I can do nothing about what's happened and the way I've been treated, I still need to face the facts and deal with the reality. I've learned that most of us keep things hidden and tell ourselves the stories that we want to hear because we're either not ready, or we're unwilling, to deal with the real issue. It's hard work to face the things that we've been avoiding, it's emotionally draining and sometimes difficult to see what rewards there are for us at the end of the process.

We have to admit that we've been lying to ourselves and unpick all of the reasons behind why we've done that. We have to decide 'why' we want to challenge our thinking. Ask ourselves what we hope to achieve by dredging up thoughts and memories that we may have buried to protect ourselves. And once we've done that, we have to make sure that we're ready to take the first step towards the things that we want and the way that we want to feel.

It took me a long time to work out why challenging the stories I'd been telling myself was so important. I needed to face facts to allow me to move on with my life. I'd been holding myself back and realising that the first step to being able to be my authentic self was to stop lying to myself about how much pain and sadness I was holding inside.

It's a work in progress and, like I say, I still feel sad at times. But I can handle that now because I know that my life isn't pointless. Everything that's happened over the course of my life is done. Those experiences are now just memories. Memories that I can choose to learn from. And by recognising that, I now live a life where my focus is enabling myself and those around me to flourish.

Purpose

My reason for being, in other words my personal purpose, is to stimulate reflection, inspire belief and ignite growth to enable myself and those around me to flourish. Now, this may sound a little 'pie in sky' to you. It's all well and good saying this stuff, but how do you actually make it happen? Before we get on to how I make this happen for myself and those around me, we need to look at how we find our purpose in the first place. I can tell you now, from my experience it doesn't simply drop into your lap. It wasn't a quick process for me, it took a lot of time, effort, commitment, and some deep thinking before I decided that this was my reason to get out of bed in the morning.

I know when I was struggling to see the point of my life (and believe me there were times when the only reason to get out of bed was to go to the loo) I hated the people who seemed to have it all worked out. The people who would say that you just need to put in the effort and you'll reap the rewards. That's much easier said than done, and we're not all in a position where we are ready to put the work in. I realise now that I've always had the potential to be happy and to bring hope to others, but maybe I just wasn't ready for it earlier in my life. Something obviously wasn't right for me, I don't know what that was, maybe I was 'happy' playing the victim. It's much easier to accept that things are happening to you, that people are making you feel a particular way, that it's 'just the way I am', that it's 'fate' and there's nothing you can do about it. Because once we realise that we can take control and we can choose our responses to the events that we've experienced, we then have the difficult decision to make as to whether we actually want to take control. But once we decide it is what we want we can then commit to all of the work that comes with taking responsibility for our thoughts and actions.

I mentioned earlier that I'm not a big believer in quick wins. Anything that's worth having, and we're talking here about your reason for living – which is a pretty big thing – takes work, hard work. To make sustainable change takes time and effort and you have to know the reason why it's important to you. But once you work that out, and have your purpose fixed in your mind, there's nothing that will knock you off track because, if defined correctly and authentically, your purpose will act as your guiding light in all that you do. Once you know why you do what you do, and why that is so important to you, your resilience will grow and you'll begin to feel a little less stuck. And once you're able to begin to wriggle free of the constraints that have been holding you back, you'll see the endless possibilities that the world holds for you.

When we feel stuck our thoughts keep us trapped in a world full of closed doors and darkness. Imagine yourself in a dark room. There are no windows and a single door in the corner. You've never seen the door open. You have no idea what is behind the door and have stopped trying to imagine what may be on the other side. You've resigned yourself to a life in the dark, and over time you get used to it. You feel safe in the confines of the dark room. There's nothing to hurt you. Nothing to be scared of. It's easy to sit and think of nothing. Then one day the door opens, but only for a second or two. Bright light shines in, revealing a colourful pattern on the wall opposite to where you're sitting. Then it's dark again. But you have changed. You can't unsee the colourful pattern on the wall. You only had a glimpse but you're curious. You wonder what it is. You hope that the door opens again soon so you can get a better look. The next day the door opens, and remains open for a few minutes allowing you to study the pattern. At first it just seems like random blobs of colour, but as your eyes adjust you realise that it's a landscape painting. The door closes and the painting disappears. The following day the door stays open for an hour. You get up close to the painting, taking in all of the details, the brush strokes, the varying shades of green in the trees and the grass, the figure in the distance, and the reflection of clouds in the still water of the lake. The door closes and you begin to wonder whether that is a painting of a real place. Your mind starts to race. You start to think about where it might be. And what else there may be beyond the closed door. You can't wait for the door to open again so you can take a step outside to see what the world looks like with your own eyes. You're excited. And maybe a little scared.

Stepping out of what you're used to can be scary but once we begin to open our mind to the possibilities of what might be out there, the benefits of taking that step soon outweigh the perceived risks. Once we realise that there's more to life than what we can see at this moment we start to think differently. And when we're feeling stuck, thinking differently is good.

10. Believe; In endless possibilities

"If you give people a chance, they shine."
Billy Connolly

I've felt stuck more times than I can remember. Stuck in dead-end jobs, stuck in a mood, stuck in a mindset, and stuck in the past, and I've realised over the years that the only person keeping me there was me. I never gave myself a chance. But once I started to shift my energy away from the negatives, I slowly began to see that life is full of possibilities. Once I stopped looking for shit all of the time, I began to see that the world offers hope and the chance to live a different life if we're prepared to give things a go.

I used to believe that everything was someone else's fault. I didn't want to take responsibility for my life. A while ago I decided that instead of viewing my life through the lens of someone feeling like the victim; instead of believing that I'd never be happy or successful, instead of waiting for good things to happen to me, and instead of looking down at my feet and not taking control, I needed to start to look up. And so I did, one evening when I was feeling particularly stuck I stepped outside into the back garden and looked up at the sky. It was just starting to go dark and the sky was clear. The moon was shining brightly and a few stars were beginning to appear and I remember feeling very small and insignificant. That feeling of insignificance increased as I stared into the ever-growing darkness of space but it felt strangely empowering. It wasn't a 'worthlessness' feeling of insignificance, more of a realisation that I was spending my life stuck in my own head and that I was wasting my time focusing my energy on things that were bringing no value, no pleasure, and no hope to my life.

Look up

I continue to 'look up' whenever I'm beginning to feel overwhelmed or stuck in my life. Regardless of the time of day or night, the weather, or where I am in the world, this practice acts as a bit of grounding for me. Whether it's feeling the warmth of the sun on my face, watching the geese fly arrow-like across the sky, searching out the brightest star, watching the snow fall from the clouds, or allowing myself to be immersed in the pouring rain, looking up helps me to believe that there is a universe of possibilities out there to explore and discover; as long as I don't get lost in my own head.

As a coach I act as a mirror to the people I'm working with. I help to raise awareness within them of the challenges they're facing by reflecting their thoughts, words and actions back to them. And this is the approach I've taken with myself over the years. I've had to dig deep to recognise how I'm feeling and what I'd like the alternatives to be, and it's these 'looking up' moments that have helped to shift my mindset from one of negativity, to a mindset of possibility.

I realised that I'd spent my life looking down. Looking down on myself, looking down at the floor to avoid eye-contact with anyone, looking down to remain invisible; but that hadn't served me very well at all. I'd been full of self-doubt, possessing the most negative mindset that kept me stuck, and by starting to look up instead I began to realise that there were opportunities to change who I was. Or more accurately, change my perceptions of who I thought I was. I realised that every time I met somebody new I could be a version of myself that I really wanted to be. They didn't know me or my history so what was there to lose? And so I started to act a little more confidently (fake it till you make it is a real thing in my experience). Rather than saying things like 'I'm not sure,' or 'I don't think so...', I'd say things like, 'I'll give it a try,' and 'Yes, I'd like to be involved.' Instead of shying away in group settings I'd put myself forward for tasks, speak up a little more, and share my ideas as I eased myself into my 'new' skin. And do you know what, before I knew it those behaviours were coming naturally to me and people began to ask me to get involved in more and more things, which, in turn, helped to build my confidence and enabled me to move on to building my self-worth in other areas of my life.

You have to 'do' to become confident, but 'doing' takes confidence, and it's often quite difficult to get going. This is where you need to believe and trust in the process. If you do nothing, nothing will change, but in my experience, as soon as you start to take those tiny steps, a whole world of possibilities can open up for you.

I clearly remember a conversation with my wife, Tracy, not long after we met that helped me start to put things into perspective and to begin to become unstuck. I was feeling sorry for myself (as was often the case) over nothing in particular. I'd got myself into a 'spiral.' In other words I'd gradually allowed my mood to get darker and darker. I said earlier in the book that I've never been diagnosed with depression, but I've had some very low moments in my life; and spiralling had become a bit of a habit that I'd gotten into. Often it would be something trivial that would trigger it, then I'd look for anything and everything that was going wrong, always referring back to my childhood experiences. I'd deliberately focus on the bad, sometimes starting an argument, often being a complete dick. It was during one of these 'spiralling' episodes that Tracy said to me; "Imagine yourself on the moon looking back at the earth. Look at how big the world is. Imagine how many people there are going through trauma of some kind at this very moment. What would they give to be in your shoes today?"

I knew pretty much from the moment we met that Tracy was very special. She 'got' me and I trusted her with everything. I was happy to be my most vulnerable with her and she's repaid me with honesty, kindness, love, support, and many moments that have helped to bring clarity to my otherwise messed up mind. Her intent has always been to help me to see in myself what she sees. She has always had belief in me, faith in my ability to be a better person, and in my potential to make a difference to the world. And that comment about where I stood at that moment in time is a perfect example of how she could cut through my spiralling dark moods and help me to see the reality of my situation; which was that I had a job, we were in a new relationship, I had a house, two lovely children. And importantly, that my abuse had ended about 15 years earlier.

She wasn't for a second trivialising what I'd been though or telling me to 'get a grip.' What she was doing was helping me to see that, in that moment, I was in a good place. I was in the kind of place that I'd have given anything to be in when I was being abused. I was safe and I was with somebody who liked me for who I was (moods and all). But too often I was allowing my past to dominate my present and my future; and in that moment I knew it had to change. Slowly I began to believe that I could be somebody. Not necessarily somebody who was rich and famous. Just somebody who could be happy with who I was. Somebody who Tracy and my children could be proud of. Somebody who could make a difference in the world. I didn't know how it would all happen, but I slowly began to believe that it could happen. And that was enough to get me started.

11. Be the person you always knew you were

"A lot of people say that it's a lack of vocabulary that makes you swear. Rubbish. I know thousands of words but I still prefer 'fuck.'" Billy Connolly

I love pretty much everything about Billy Connolly. His story is an inspiration to me, his on-stage performances and TV shows have brought me so much joy over the years and now I have a couple of limited edition pieces of his art hanging on the walls of my home (with plans to add more hopefully). He has been a constant in my life since I was a teenager. I've seen him live a couple of times; around 30 years apart. The first time I saw him he was bouncing around the stage, full of energy. I was in awe of how one person could fill a stage and command the attention of so many people. The second time was during his final stand-up tour, and although his physical energy was very different to the first time I saw him due to the effects of Parkinson's disease, which saw him standing next to a small table in the centre of the stage for the whole show, he still managed to captivate the audience with his presence. On both occasions that I was lucky enough to be in the same space as him, Billy had us all in the palm of his hand, hanging on his every word, and I remember walking out of the theatres feeling like I'd spent an evening with a good friend. He'd told his stories, had me in fits of laughter, and made me feel part of his world. I think that's why I love him so much (not in a strange, stalker kind of way obviously), he makes me feel welcome and I'll be forever grateful for that. From the first time that I saw Billy Connolly he's made me feel like I belong. He is somebody who I've looked up to, he is unashamedly himself, he is brilliant at all that he does, yet he seems so humble and down-to-earth. All things that I aspire to be.

It's hard to explain why I feel the way I do about him as I don't completely understand it myself. I just know that whenever I see him on TV or listen to him talking, he brings a smile to my face. And I suppose that's the important thing here. Recognising what brings you joy and filling your life with as much of that stuff as possible is key to helping us overcome any challenges we may have. Life can be hard, and I'm not saying for a second that it's easy to overcome our challenges but there's no doubting that if we look for shit, we're certain to find it; so surely it goes without saying that if we search for joy, fun, and laughter, there's a pretty good chance we'll find that too. Billy has taught me to see life for what it is. Something that we only get one shot at, something that is to be enjoyed, not endured, and something that we have complete control over. Regardless of what is going on around us, we can choose to see things from a different angle. We can see the funny side of even the most serious situations, we can take lessons from even our toughest challenges, and we always have the opportunity to 'reinvent' ourselves at any given moment and be the person we always wanted to be.

Thinking about how Billy has gone from working in the shipyards, playing the banjo in small settings, progressing to TV and huge venues as a comedian, starring in movies and becoming a renowned artist is a constant inspiration to me. It shows how we are constantly changing and growing and that we need to embrace all of what is important to us, and to live our lives doing the things that bring us joy.

I struggled for years to try and pin down what I wanted to 'be' and that brought a fair bit of turmoil to my life. It was horrible feeling stuck in jobs that didn't generate any kind of spark within me, and it was only when I stopped trying to find my perfect job and thinking about what I wanted to be, and instead started focusing on how I wanted to feel that things began to change for me.

I realised that I need to feel valued, that I want to contribute positively to as many peoples' lives as possible, and that it's crucial that I can be my authentic self in any situation I find myself in. These realisations took a lot of finding as for so many years I'd believed that to be 'successful' was to be wealthy financially. I'm not saying that wealth isn't (or shouldn't be) a measure of success if that suits you. And we all know that we need money to live, to pay our bills, to keep a roof over our heads and to do some of the things that bring us joy, but I truly believe that if we focus solely on making money and have that as our main driver, we're in danger of missing out on discovering what our true purpose is.

Just to remind you, my purpose is to stimulate reflection, inspire belief, and ignite growth to enable myself and those around me to flourish. And understanding how I want to feel, combined with living life with my purpose in mind has really changed the way I look at my existence. Having these clear goals in mind helps me to live a life on my terms and to power through any challenges and setbacks that I now face. Instead of trying to work out where I fit into society or feeling worthless and invisible, I now have a clear vision of who I am, and why doing what I do is important to me.

A big thing for me throughout my life has been a lack of confidence and low (sometimes no) self-worth but that didn't have to be the case for as long as it was. On reflection if I'd listened to my heart earlier in my life I would have heard that my values have always centred around being kind. But I didn't take the time to listen as I was too busy feeling sorry for myself. So I floated through life, not considering what it was all about, why I was here, and what was important to me. Basically, I spent a lot of time not thinking.

I've learned that by not thinking and just floating through life I wasn't seeing my value as a unique individual with endless potential. I wasn't committed to anything, I didn't take pride in anything that I achieved, I didn't have a voice, I didn't value myself, I didn't see my worth, I didn't understand that it was okay to want to feel happy, loved, and content, and I didn't ever feel that I deserved kindness from anybody (including myself). And I don't want any of that for you.

12. Allow yourself to live

"The biggest troublemaker you'll probably ever have to deal with watches you shave his face in the mirror every morning." Cowboy proverb

I was 28 when Kenny died. It was the third brain tumour that got him. We'd known each other for eleven years, we'd worked together as fitted-kitchen makers when we were seventeen and hit it off straight away. We were drinking partners, football buddies, piss-takers and all the things that best mates are supposed to be. But we never really talked, not properly, not about anything important. It was all about having a laugh, getting drunk and watching the match. It took me a long time to get over losing Kenny. I still think about him regularly more than twenty years later. I wonder what he'd be doing, who he'd be with, whether he'd have children or not, whether or not we'd still be mates or if our lives might have gone off on different tangents. Who knows.

We have all been through challenging times. Some more so than others, but every single one of us has had to deal with something in our past. But how many of us can leave it there? As

I said, it took me ages to get over my friend's death, we were really close and, at the time I thought I'd never have a mate like him again. Even though I'd never opened up about my past to him, he somehow just 'got' me and I felt a little less invisible when I was around him.

But do you know what, there are lots of great people out there and I've been fortunate enough to get to know and make friends with loads of them. And I have to mention a very special person in my life at this point. When Kenny died I lost my best mate and I never thought I'd find a friendship with another man that was as strong. But around the same time that I met Tracy, Warren Thomas came into my life. We worked together for a couple of years, before I moved on to a new job. We hit it off straight away, always chatting and laughing throughout our shifts together and our friendship has lasted the test of time. We've been on holidays together, seen one another's children grow up, shared countless 'tipsy' evenings, and welcomed in our fair share of new years with each other… and I'm so proud to say that I'm honoured to be his Best Man when he marries his gorgeous bride-to-be Michelle in July 2023.

But the friendship with Warren (and others) might not have happened if I'd allowed myself to stay rooted to the past. Letting go of the emotions that held Kenny so close to me felt a bit like a betrayal. I'm not really sure what I mean by that, but I think some of it was around feeling guilty. There were definite feelings of regret for the future, of what might have been for him and for us as friends, there was obvious hurt, sorrow and anger. Why him, he was only young, he'd got his whole life ahead of him. And there was also a huge feeling of 'why me?'

Why do bad things always happen to me? It's because it's me. This is just my luck. I found a mate who I could (almost) be myself with and he was taken away. I'm obviously not meant to be happy. It's because I'm worthless.

This kind of destructive self-talk has been a huge part of 'me' since childhood and my mate's death just helped to amplify it even more. It felt like the end of the world. Because of his death everything in the world was bad and it was just a matter of time before my world completely crumbled. Somehow it felt like it was my fault. The whole scenario played into my belief that I shouldn't be happy or have anything to look forward to. I'd been told it for years, it was part of who I was, and I might as well just accept it and get on with living a worthless life.

How often have you had disempowering thoughts like these? When something goes wrong do you blame yourself or catastrophise as I did? How often do you question your self-worth or see everything as black and white; it's either good or it's bad with no in-between?

These are common thinking 'errors' or, to give them a technical name, cognitive distortions. Regardless of what they're called, when this kind of thinking goes unchecked, it can very often lead to feelings of overwhelm, stress, anxiety and depression. Believing everything our brain is telling us is not always the most helpful way to live our lives. If we take my experience as an example, looking back it's now obvious to me that what I'd been told throughout my childhood had stuck in my head. I'd never challenged the way I thought and when things went wrong (as they often do in life) my default setting was to drop into victim mode and feel sorry for myself.

I was convinced, although I now realise that I'd never properly thought about it, that what I was thinking was true. In my mind I was worthless, I shouldn't be happy and I'd never be anything. But the reality was very different. I was a dad, I had a job, I was married, and owned a house. But none of that seemed to register. All of the helpful stuff slipped away too easily, leaving me with a mind full of negative, disempowering, unhelpful, destructive thoughts. The American psychologist, Rick Hanson says;

"The brain is like Velcro for negative experiences, but Teflon for positive ones."

And when we consider that we all have a negativity bias (we naturally look for the bad stuff), it's no surprise that we can often see the world, our lives, our relationships, our abilities, and our potential in a very dim light.

But how accurate a reflection is that? How much of what we think is true, how much is based on facts and evidence? And how much is based on our assumptions, on our feelings, or on guesswork? In relation to my friend's death, the reality was that he had a series of brain tumours that, regardless of what I did, who I was, and what I'd been through, I had absolutely no control over. There was nothing I could have done to change the situation. It didn't happen because of the things that I'd been through, or the way that I'd been treated. It was a very sad, very tragic way to lose a very good friend.

And when I think back to all of the laughs we had together I'll be forever grateful for the time that Kenny was in my life. I've said for years that I believe everything happens for a reason but I'm not sure about that anymore. To believe that might mean to believe in fate; to somehow believe that this life is all pre-planned out for us and that regardless of what we do, we'll end up where we were always supposed to be. I don't know if I can accept that. As I'm getting older I'm realising just how much control I do have over my life; and always have had, if I'd only taken the time to think about it.

Everything begins and ends in my head. My experiences, negative self-talk, and my assumptions have influenced the way I've approached life; often resulting in not very positive outcomes for me. But now I understand that I have complete control over my emotions, and that I have the power to decide how I want to respond in any given situation. I feel liberated and free to be myself and live a life on my terms. A life where I decide where I go, what I do, and how I feel.

I may not believe in fate, but what I do believe in is that people come into our lives for a reason. We cross paths with so many people over the course of our lives and every single one of them brings something unique and offers us an opportunity to learn something new. In my experience, that something new has often been about myself.

Kenny taught me to not take life too seriously. He made me realise that having wavy shoulder-length hair didn't suit me, encouraging me to have it all shaved off... something I've done ever since, although now I have no choice as I'm the proud owner of a bald head! He showed me the importance of standing up for yourself, he was no shrinking violet and spoke up whenever he felt like he was being wronged. He taught me that I could be liked for who I am. And his untimely death taught me that I have always been resilient. I was heart-broken when he went, but like the years of abuse that I'd suffered, it didn't break me. Looking back, I may have always had something inside me, pushing me through the challenges I was facing but, if I'm honest, I think I was just too scared to admit that I was struggling and, like the abuse, I swept my emotions under the carpet. Something I now understand, is not the most helpful thing to do. That pile of crap doesn't go away, it just keeps getting bigger and bigger until you begin to trip over it on a regular basis. Unless dealt with and 'cleaned up' those thoughts and emotions hold you back from being your true authentic self. Throughout my life I've found myself pretending to be happy-go-lucky, pasting a smile on my face and saying that everything is okay, when a lot of the time I've just wanted to curl up in a ball and cry.

Alcohol 'helped' with keeping up that front; I'd like to think I've never had a problem with drinking but when I look back whenever I went out I always drank to excess. I thought that booze brought out the best in me. I felt free and confident. I took the dance floor by storm and all the ladies wanted to be with me. In reality I was making a dick of myself; where I thought my dancing was enhanced by the lubricating and liberating effects of Snakebites and Southern Comfort chasers, the fact was that I was stumbling around and pogoing to anything and everything, desperately looking around the club at kicking out time for somebody to show me a flicker of affection. Writing this down brings back many embarrassing memories, and even more hazy recollections of bar fights and drunken liaisons with nameless women. All of which are things I'm not particularly proud of, but all happened and all offer valuable life lessons.

All of the lessons from Kenny (apart from the hair-cutting) have been slow-burners. What I mean by that is that he planted the seeds in my mind that things could be different, but for a very long time I didn't water those seeds. Looking back, I don't think I realised what I was being taught. Maybe I wasn't ready to think differently. I still saw myself as a victim, and let's face it, my life hadn't been a bundle of fun up to that point so those seeds sat in the infertile mud of my mind. They were never nurtured or given the opportunity to grow. But gradually over the years, I began to feed those seeds, and with the help of Tracy, they are now flourishing for everyone to see.

"Don't cry because it's over. Smile because it happened."
Dr. Seuss

LAGOM

JUST THE RIGHT AMOUNT...
NOT TOO LITTLE,
AND NOT TOO MUCH

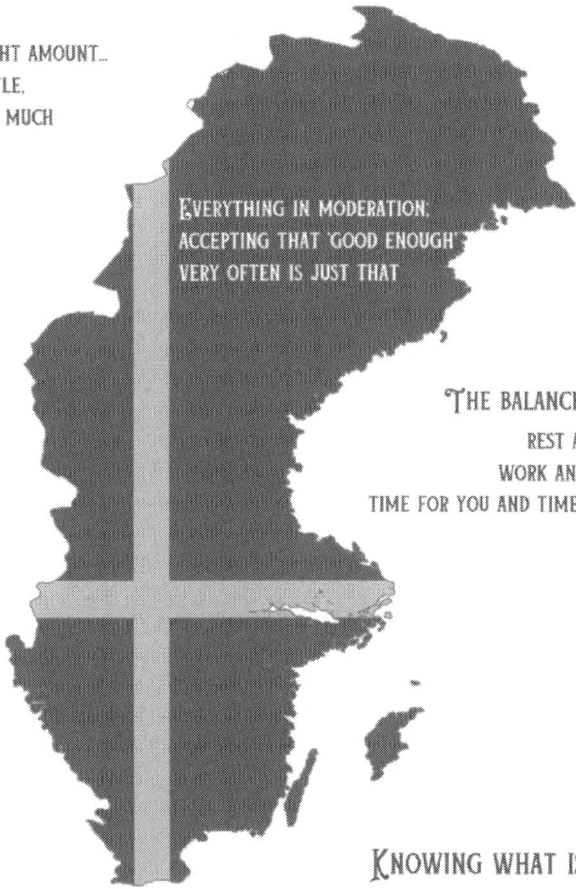

EVERYTHING IN MODERATION;
ACCEPTING THAT 'GOOD ENOUGH'
VERY OFTEN IS JUST THAT

THE BALANCE BETWEEN:
REST AND EXERCISE
WORK AND HOME LIFE
TIME FOR YOU AND TIME FOR OTHERS

KNOWING WHAT IS ENOUGH

SWEDEN

13. What is happiness anyway?

"When people say 'it's always the last place you look.' Of course it is. Why would you keep looking after you've found it?" Billy Connolly

The idea of happiness and the thought of being happy is right up there on the list of things that most of us crave. Happiness is different for everyone and it comes in all shapes and sizes. You might have a favourite smell that reminds you of a happy time, a particular song that makes you smile, a 'happy' place that you love to visit, or a good feeling that you get when you're around certain people. But how often do you stop and take in that moment? When was the last time you really thought about what happiness means to you?

Life is just a series of moments. Moments to live, moments to experience, and moments to learn from. According to the psychologist Robert Plutchik[11], we have the capacity to 'feel' over 34,000 emotions and why would we be able to do that if joy and happiness were all we were supposed to experience? But joy and happiness are the things we're told that we need to find if we are to be fulfilled and content. They are sold to us as the Holy Grail of emotions and that without them our lives are almost meaningless. But how helpful is that?

If we're constantly searching for happiness, aren't we just setting ourselves up to fail most of the time? And if we're always searching for joy, how many experiences and emotions are we missing out on? I spent years focussing on this 'mythical' emotion called happiness and it did me no favours whatsoever.

Chasing a life chock-full of 'happiness' by ignoring all our other emotions could, ironically, lead to us never finding what we're striving for. If we expect every moment of every day to be filled with joyous laughter, sunshine and smiling faces, we're likely to be disappointed. I should know, I was very unhappy for years. A big part of that was feeling like I had no control over what was going on in my life. I've already touched on the power of realising that you, and you alone, are in control of how you want to feel in any given circumstance. And as empowering as that is, if you don't know how you want to feel, how will you ever know when you've reached what you've been looking for?

Let me try and explain by using the concept of happiness as an example. You may have noticed that I called happiness a 'mythical' emotion a little earlier in this chapter and the reason for that is that happiness, in my experience, was an emotion that, for a very long time, lived only in my imagination. I never defined what happiness meant to me and spent my life saying things like, 'I don't want much, I just want to be happy.' But what did that actually mean?

It's easy to say 'I want to be happy', but how often do we actually break that down and analyse what happiness actually means for us as individuals. It's easy to say that you want it, but unless you've defined what it is for you as an individual how do you know what you're looking for; and how will you know when you've found it, and are feeling it? It feels like 'happiness' should be a universal emotion that is the same for everyone. The way the word is bandied about and the means in which the concept is 'sold' to us can make us feel that if we're not happy there is something wrong with us, and that we need fixing.

But what definition of happiness are 'they' working to? If we're chasing somebody else's version or definition what chance do we have of finding it? But by defining what it is we're hoping to get, by thinking through what our version of happiness is, and by imagining how it will feel to be happy, we'll recognise the positive steps we're taking towards it and will know when we've found it; and will no longer feel the need to keep looking.

We're all individuals, with our very own window on the world. We all have different things that make us smile, that bring us joy, that make us 'happy.' So when we throw it out there that we want to be happy, what does that actually mean? I know that I spent a lot of years desperate to be 'happy' but looking back I had no idea what I actually wanted. I'd say the words and hope for the best. But how was I ever going to find what I was looking for, if I didn't have the first idea what that was? Talk about looking for a needle in a haystack. Over the last 20 or so years I've done a lot of work on myself and am now pretty confident I know what happiness means to me. So here goes:

Happiness is giving, sharing, inspiring, and learning. But it is also a cold cider on a sunny day, a red wine on a winter's evening, a good single malt to end a busy Saturday. It is fish and chips by the seaside, a roast beef dinner, a North Indian garlic chilli chicken curry with naan bread, and enjoying a Spanish Paella in Madrid. Happiness is reading a book in the garden, walking by the canal with my dog, laughing with my wife at something silly, and watching a good drama box set. Happiness is sitting around the dinner table with my family. It's knowing that you don't have to get up early but waking up anyway and just relaxing with a coffee. It is family, friends, holidays and parties; it's appreciating what we have and… I could go on. But the point that I'm making is that happiness is all of these things and more for me.

Why not spend a bit of time making a list of all the things that make you happy? Maybe create a vision board or mind map, use the 'Notes' function on your phone; whatever works for you. Add to it whenever something makes you smile, and don't just think about the big stuff. Yes, get started with your obvious ones, but be sure to make a note of the tiniest things too. In our downstairs loo we have a couple of quotes that hang on the wall. My favourite of the two is "Some days we have to make our own sunshine." Nothing could be more true, as I've already said (and will continue to repeat), nobody apart from you has the power to make you feel any way that you don't want to feel. If we rely on others for our happiness and wellbeing we could be waiting forever. We have everything we need inside us to be our 'own sunshine' and just the realisation of that was enough for me to make a few fundamental changes that set me on the path to becoming a coach, mentor, and 'happy'.

"To compare is to despair." Victoria Etchells

Whilst searching for our happiness it's important not to compare ourselves to others, especially in an age where social media rules and we don't know whether what we see being shared is true, a massive exaggeration, or a complete fabrication. We have to be careful not to fall into the trap of thinking that we 'should' be feeling a certain way just because it looks like everybody else is. We have to be authentic and true to ourselves and live our lives in a way that suits us, and in a way that brings us our version of happiness.

I've done a bit of research on happiness concepts from around the world and thought this would be as good a place as any to share some of my findings. The following are ideas that I've found by simply Googling (other search engines are available) and following a few links. If any of the ideas take your fancy, why not take a little more time to research and see how they could bring you the happiness you deserve?

So what does happiness mean to you? Before I share the concepts of happiness from around the world, take some time to answer these questions:

1. **When I'm at my happiest, I am…**
2. **The last time I felt truly happy I was…**

As you read through the various concepts of happiness from around the world think about the following questions:

1. **What are your first thoughts about the concept?**

2. **What might you take from it to help bring you more happiness?**

3. **How would incorporating this idea (or bits of this idea) add to what is already good in your life?**

In alphabetical order – here we go:

Azart (Russia) Excitement

Azart is all about taking risks and getting joy from living life to the fullest. Taking life by the horns, thrill-seeking and finding excitement and passion in activities that others may find terrifying and be uncomfortable with.

Buen Vivir (Ecuador) Good living

Living the 'good life' means that you see yourself as part of something bigger. Community and family are at the centre of Buen Vivir, as well as looking after the environment. A greater focus on slowing down, appreciating what you have, and enjoying experiences over possessions.

Craic (Ireland) A good time: friendly, lively talk

The focus here is all on having a good time. Laughing, joking and loud conversations are the order of the day. Making time for fun with friends, being sociable and enjoying yourself... particularly on a night out.

Entrückt (Germany) Entranced

If you are Entrückt you could be said to be lost in thought. It's about being comfortable in your own company, daydreaming, meditating, and enjoying the calm that peace and quiet brings.

Estrenar (Spain) Brand new

How good does it feel when you use or wear something for the first time? Maybe it's the confidence that new pair of shoes give you, the pleasure of your new PJs, the feel of new bedclothes, or setting up your new phone. Estrenar is all about that feeling.

Fare la bella figura (Italy) Make the beautiful figure

This Italian concept is all about being your best self to live a happier life. The idea is that if you make a good impression on the world by the way you look and act you will be rewarded. Being kind, tactful, graceful, respectful and considerate of others is as important as looking 'beautiful.'

Fika (Sweden) Coffee

Fika is much more than coffee. It's about setting time aside for (at least one) daily break and is best experienced with others. Fika is about slowing things down, and taking the time to savour a hot drink, something sweet and good conversation.

Flâner (France) To stroll

Just walking and taking in your surroundings is the name of the game here. Take your time, leisurely stroll and let your feet guide you. Throw away the agenda and guidebook and simply enjoy the sights, sounds, smells and surprises along the way.

Friluftsliv (Norway) Outdoor life

Create a connection to nature by being in nature. Friluftsliv is all about achieving a state of mind and 'being' outdoors rather than 'doing' outdoors. It's about appreciating all that the outdoors has to offer and 'being' in the moment.

Gemütlichkeit (Germany) Cosiness

Being together with friends and family, celebrating and enjoying each other's company. Creating feelings of warmth, contentment and belonging. Sharing food, drink and good times, and showing gratitude for the special people in your life.

Gezelligheid (The Netherlands) Conviviality

The quality of being friendly and lively; friendliness.

Create special moments effortlessly by enjoying the small things in life. This happiness concept is about doing the things that make you feel good, whilst sharing your time with others. It's about companionship, togetherness and friendships; and being sociable, comfortable and relaxed.

Guyub (Indonesia)

Guyub is all about social connections, a strong sense of belonging, solid support networks, and compassion for one another. Selfless acts of kindness, sincerely taking pleasure in the good fortune of others, and knowing that you matter to those around you is at the heart of Guyub.

Ho'oponopono (Hawaii)

This Hawaiian concept has its roots in forgiveness and reconciliation. The idea is that resentment towards others mostly does harm to your own happiness and wellbeing. It's about developing self-awareness and reflecting on your thoughts and feelings before talking (and working) it through to resolution.

Hygge (Denmark)

The quality of being warm and comfortable that gives a feeling of happiness. Hygge is all about being comfortable enough to be you, in a space that makes you comfortable; enjoying the familiar, revelling in the company of good friends, feeling safe and able to let go of your cares and creating personal spaces for you to be 'you.'

Kalsarikännit (Finland) Translation: Buttocks

I love this translation. Another description of this Finnish concept of happiness is 'drinking at home in your underwear with no intention of going out.' It's all about that feeling when you simply want to stay at home, make no effort, and enjoy some 'me time.'

KALSARIKÄNNIT

WHEN YOU WANT TO:
STAY AT HOME
MAKE NO EFFORT
ENJOY SOME 'ME' TIME

'DRINKING AT HOME IN YOUR UNDERWEAR WITH NO INTENTION OF GOING OUT.'

FINLAND

Keyif (Turkey) Pleasure

Practising mindfulness, relaxing and living in the moment. Keyif is about finding the time and space to enjoy some quiet time, whether that be five minutes or an hour or two. It's about relaxing, recharging and resetting before heading back to your busy life.

Lagom (Sweden) Moderate

Lagom is all about having just the right amount; not too little, and not too much. It's everything in moderation; accepting that 'good enough' very often is just that. It's the balance between rest and exercise, between work and home life, between taking time for yourself and making time for others. It's about knowing what is enough.

Lykke (Denmark) Happiness

This Danish concept is about embracing the idea that happiness is all around you. It's about having more experiences and less stuff, and finding your version of freedom. Lykke is an attitude, it's about looking at your life and considering what little things you can change here and there to bring you more joy.

Meraki (Greece)

"When you leave a piece of yourself, your soul, creativity, and love in what you do. To put a little bit of yourself into something."

It's a labour of love, it's about gaining happiness from giving your undivided attention to a task; especially something like cooking, or getting creative. Make the time to concentrate on one task at a time (no multitasking allowed).

Niksen (The Netherlands) Nothing

Niksen is the art of doing nothing! It's about allowing your mind to wander, giving yourself the freedom to not think, and to just allow what will be, to be. It's about relaxing into your surroundings and just 'being', without any purpose at all.

Pakikipagkapwa-tao (Philippines) Interpersonal skills

This concept of happiness is all about being more empathetic, conscious of the needs of others, and being part of a community who are all willing to help each other out, regardless of whether there's a direct benefit to them or not. It's about relating to each other as equals, being loving, helpful and selfless.

Petta Reddast (Iceland)

Positive thinking is the main ingredient of Petta Reddast. It's believing that everything will work out okay. Accepting that things don't always go to plan but you always have the power to decide how you want to feel. It's about having a sense of perspective, accepting your feelings and asking yourself what small things you can do in this moment that will begin to change things.

Pura Vida (Costa Rica) Pure life

Pura Vida is a way of life, an attitude. It's enjoying the 'simple' things and finding small moments of happiness in all that you do. This concept of happiness focuses on the idea of enjoying life no matter what is going on for you. It's having an appreciation of life and realising that life is what you make of it.

Saudade (Brazil) Longing

This one is a little different from the rest as the focus here is on a longing for a happiness that once was. It's a feeling of nostalgia and melancholy. This 'sadness' brings feelings of happiness when good memories are recounted. It's difficult to explain but it seems that being able to experience Saudade brings its own kind of happiness.

Shinrin – Yoku (Japan) Forest well

Otherwise known as 'forest bathing' this Japanese concept is another example of how getting outside can boost your happiness levels. Shinrin-Yoku is about taking a leisurely walk in a forest or woodland and spending time amongst the trees. Being fully present in the moment, listening to the sounds of the forest, looking closely at the leaves, noticing the feelings underfoot as you wander aimlessly through the trees.

Sisu (Finland) Content

Sisu is about getting on with things, avoiding procrastination and having the strength to face difficult situations head-on. It's about getting comfortable with being uncomfortable, showing resilience, tenacity and courage, and having the determination to put one foot in front of the other when faced with tough challenges.

Tachles (Israel) Touchless

Getting straight to the point and not beating around the bush is the name of the game here. It's all about being more assertive, honest and sharing your opinions clearly; saying what you actually feel and think rather than being passive aggressive. It's about being serious, practical, and being able to achieve a purpose.

Ubuntu (South Africa)

"The idea that people are not only individuals but live in a community and must share things and care for each other."

Ubuntu is a term that translates to "I am, because you are." Compassion, mindfulness, fairness, acts of forgiveness, selflessness, and sympathy are all encouraged, along with the idea that we are all connected and our actions affect everyone.

Wabi-Sabi (Japan)

The Japanese art of finding perfection in the imperfect.

Accepting that things are not forever, and embracing things in their most natural state. It's an appreciation for the fleeting and the imperfect. It's about appreciating the beauty in the imperfections, impermanence and incompleteness of everything that's around us. Things don't need to be perfect, permanent, or complete to bring happiness.

Wu wei (China) Without effort

Wu wei is about letting go of your ego, going with the flow, and allowing other people to influence the decisions you make. It's about not taking every opportunity that comes your way, waiting before acting, delegating to others, and being selfless. It's about taking the time to breathe.

As established earlier, happiness is different for all of us. But looking at the various 'happiness' concepts from around the world we can see some common themes including:

- An ability to 'switch off'
- Treating others well
- Practising gratitude
- Taking responsibility
- Being part of something bigger
- Living in the present
- Being resilient
- A connection to nature
- Having a sense of belonging

- Enjoying your own company
- Being kind to yourself
- Having a positive outlook
- Seeing challenge as opportunity
- Living a balanced life
- Having good relationships with others.

How many of these can you relate to?

Where are the gaps that you'd like to fill?

What might you need to start (or stop) doing to bring more happiness to your life?

HO'OPONOPONO

FORGIVENESS AND RECONCILIATION

RESENTMENT TOWARDS OTHERS MOSTLY DOES HARM TO YOUR OWN HAPPINESS AND WELLBEING

HAWAII

"Now and then it's good to pause in our pursuit of happiness and just be happy." Guillaume Apollinaire

I know that I could add a bit of all of these to my life, I especially like the idea of 'drinking at home in your underwear with no intention of going out'. I do have a few particular favourites that are helping me in my quest to live a life on my terms.

Ho'oponopono has its roots in forgiveness and reconciliation. The idea is that resentment towards others mostly does harm to your own happiness and wellbeing and I can directly relate this concept to my feelings towards the man who abused me from the age of nine until I was 15.

My abuser died in September 2012 aged 56. His obituary in the local paper said that; 'He died peacefully in his sleep... he will be sadly missed by family and friends, but fondly remembered always.' My initial reaction to reading that was who would 'fondly remember' a monster like that? And how does he get that privilege? How does he get to die peacefully when he was the cause of so much pain in my life. Surely if anybody deserved to suffer a slow, agonising death it was him. Rather than being cared for in a hospital bed surely a more fitting end for a man who so liked to dominate, to terrify, to beat and abuse would have taken place in some kind of windowless torture chamber surrounded by faceless people covered in blood, baying for him to be slayed.

He tied my hands and feet to my single metal-framed bed on many occasions. Face down and biting on my pillow, I remember clenching my bum cheeks as tightly as I could to try and stop him from forcing his way inside me. He always won. No matter how hard I tried he always had the upper hand. He was a strong, powerful man and it only took a swift punch to my kidneys or his nicotine-stained fingers gripping my inner thighs, pulling my legs apart and lifting me slightly off the bed and my resistance was gone. I had no choice but to take whatever he wanted to do to me.

So why shouldn't he have suffered a similar experience when he was on his deathbed? The torture rack sprung to mind as an appropriate start, or maybe the strappado; rope tied around his wrists and his hands behind his back, he should have been hanging from the ceiling with weights around his ankles waiting for the inevitable whipping across his bare back. Not being cared for in a hospital bed.

I wondered if he'd ever been as terrified as he made me feel. Even on his death-bed, I doubted that he was as scared of dying as I was in the moments when his anger boiled over and I couldn't breathe because of his hands around my throat. The rage that I saw in his piercing eyes as his mouth was millimetres from mine explained all that I needed to know about what this man was capable of. He had been in prison for GBH before he came into my life, and I was in absolutely no doubt that if he wanted to, he could take that violence one step further.

His cruelty towards me is something that I will never forget. Feeling terrified at the thought of what was to come on the days that he wasn't working or the nights when he'd stagger in from the working men's club or local pub. Whenever he shouted down from the bedroom to bring him up a cup of tea, the many times that he forced me to take the day off school, and the moments that he'd sneak into my bedroom while I was playing with my toys, reading, or doing my homework. I never knew what to expect but I always feared the absolute worst. I lived with that fear for six years and something like that doesn't just disappear. It stayed with me for a long time after the abuse ended, and I still have moments when I get that horrible feeling in the pit of my stomach. But is that any reason to wish him the worst death imaginable?

A few years ago I would have said that it absolutely is. But what good would it have brought me? What pleasure would I really have had knowing that he had experienced such horrors as I did at his hands? I've learned over the years that thinking like this only serves to keep the pain alive. The memories are always there to be tapped into when I choose, but the pain has subsided and is under control, and I'm not sure that it would be if I'd held on to that anger.

He never apologised for anything that he put me through, neither has my mum for that matter, and that bothered me for a long time. It was almost as if in their minds, either the abuse never happened, or that I wasn't worthy of any kind of acknowledgement of the damage they had inflicted on me. But none of that matters now. It was a horrible time in my life, and there's no doubt that I'm scarred by everything that happened to me, but what's the good of holding onto those negative emotions? I'm never going to get an apology from him now and I've given up any hope of my mum acknowledging anything that happened. It's taken a long time, and I still experience the odd moments of real sadness. Sadness of never having the comfort and support of a loving mum and dad. Sadness of having my childhood ripped away from me. Sadness that I allowed him to ruin a lot of my life.

But I've come to realise (better late than never) that I'm worth more than all of that. I deserve to be happy. I'm a good person who went through bad stuff that led me to making some not very good choices that sadly affected the people who were in my life at that time. Holding on to the hate and anger wasn't serving me well and I didn't feel that I could move past what had happened, and for a long time I was stuck in the past.

Lagom has been a key element in me finding my happiness. It is knowing what 'enough' means for me and appreciating what I have rather than always thinking that the grass is greener somewhere else. Lagom fits nicely into the principle of 'Knowing where to draw the line' in the Code of the West and I use it to help me to decide when enough is more than enough. It's helping me to think about what I need to say 'no' to and reminds me to regularly ask myself, 'If I'm saying yes to this, what am I saying no to?' I've spent a lot of time criticising myself over the years because I've never felt good enough and Lagom helps me to focus on being kind to myself.

'Enough' can relate to anything but perhaps the obvious is money and possessions. If we're not careful (and believe the adverts, influencers, and marketeers) we can go through life thinking that we'll only be happy when we have the latest phone, a new car, a bigger house, and a job with more money. Now I'm not saying that those things can't bring some kind of joy to our lives, but it's important to define for ourselves when enough is enough. How much do we want to keep pushing ourselves? How much do we actually need to earn to live the kind of life that makes us happy? How much 'stuff' do we need?

It's important here to make the distinction between 'need' and 'want.' Our needs are things that are essential; this is why it's important to define what happiness means to us as individuals as once we understand what is crucial in our quest for happiness, we can recognise when we have reached our goal. For example, I always thought that to be happy I'd need to live by the sea in a warm country. In reality, this is just a want. What I actually need to be happy is to feel valued, loved, and respected.

For me, this concept of knowing when enough is enough, has been a key part of ensuring that I keep myself on track. I use it to remind myself of what I need to live a life on my terms, and I also find it helpful as it acts as a reminder to me that I am enough! When I feel like I'm worthless and the old stories start to surface, I think about how I am good enough by thinking about the people who are most important to me and the contribution I make to their lives. If I'm good enough for Mrs Nestor, and she tells me that I am, then I'm definitely good enough for everybody else.

Wabi-Sabi is taking the time to appreciate things for how they are, even if that is for the briefest of moments. Accepting that things are not forever, and embracing things in their most natural state. It's an appreciation for the fleeting and the imperfect. It's about appreciating the beauty in the imperfections, impermanence and incompleteness of everything that's around us. Things don't need to be perfect, permanent, or complete to bring happiness.

This concept has helped me take a step back, take a breath, and to find beauty in even the tiniest of things around me. It's too easy to rush through life, racing towards the next thing but I've learned that this way of living hasn't served me very well at all. Too much of my life has been spent not living in the here and now. I've spent a lot of time looking back and blaming my past for how I feel; and I've also spent a great deal of time thinking that once I reach a certain age, get a new job, move house, earn more money, move to the coast, live abroad, write a book etc. that everything will be okay.

I spent so much time either feeling sorry for myself or dreaming of a better future (without ever doing anything about it) that I forgot to make the most of the moment that I was actually living in. Days, weeks, months and years have passed me by where I was never really there. What a shame that is. Not just for me, but for the people around me. How must it feel to be around someone who is forever blaming their past or wishing away the days until they get to a better (undefined) future with no plan of how to get there? It can't be good and it's not something that I ever want to put anybody through again, and that's one of the reasons why I try and make the most of as many moments as possible.

The past has gone, I know now that I can take positives from it and learn from it, but it will not define me. The future is yet to be decided and I now understand that no matter how much I want something or wish for it to be a reality, the only way that it will ever happen is for me to take action. And the best way to do this, is to recognise that this very moment is all we actually have. And to make the most of this time we need to define what we want, and commit to action. Those actions may not always result in what we hope to achieve, but regardless of whether things are imperfect, impermanent, or incomplete there is value to be found in everything that we do. Wabi-Sabi has taught me to enjoy all aspects of my life and embrace all that I am, and all that I offer, and to always be true to myself safe in the knowledge that even if things don't go to plan I can always reflect on what has happened and take something worthwhile from the experience.

Not only does it help me make the most of every fleeting moment, thinking about Wabi-Sabi helps me to appreciate that even when I make a mistake and am not 'perfect' in the moment, that is okay. Actually, it's more than okay. It's an opportunity to celebrate that I've tried something, and that I've not settled for how things are. It's a moment to enjoy and to recognise what I have learned about myself, and to decide what I'd like to do with that new knowledge. Oftentimes I just sit with it for a while and do nothing else. I've learned to appreciate the moment and to not beat myself up for not being perfect or getting it right first time, which is such a valuable lesson to learn and has taken so much pressure off me in so many ways.

For me, these three concepts work brilliantly in combating the negativity bias that I mentioned earlier. I just have to say here though, this hasn't been a quick fix (and is still very much a work in progress). Changing the way we think doesn't happen quickly; we have years of ingrained thought processes that need to be untangled and re-rooted; but it can be done. With time, patience, persistence, and commitment (and maybe some professional help) you can change the way you look at things, you can change the way you view your world, you can change the way you feel about yourself. You just have to want to and commit to putting in the work.

Take your time to answer the questions posed earlier in this chapter and also ask yourself which are your favourite 'happiness' concepts and why? And then decide how you might add them to your life a little bit at a time. In my experience it's so important to make small changes to ensure that they stick and become part of you. I've learned that trying to make too many changes too quickly often ended up with me back where I started. In some cases, worse off than when I started as my despair at not being able to make sustainable changes led to much harsher negative self-talk with the reinforcement of the often-told stories of me being useless and worthless making regular appearances in my mind.

"Change does not take time – it takes commitment." Thomas Crum

What does success mean to you?

While we're thinking about how to define what happiness means to us, it seems an appropriate time to discuss success too. In much the same way that I used to say that I wanted to be 'happy', I'd also dream of being 'successful'. Because, obviously, with success comes money, and with money comes happiness. But does it, does it really?

When I was younger I thought to be successful was to drive a Jaguar, live in a big house and have loads of money. And because of my feelings of uselessness and lack of self-worth, I always believed that I'd never be successful. I would never have a career that enabled me to earn lots of money and so I lived a long time feeling frustrated and angry as I was destined to never be a success. And going by the definition I gave above, I'm still not a success. I don't have loads of money, I live in a semi-detached house, and definitely don't drive a Jaguar. But that's all okay because I realised a while ago that for me, success doesn't equal lots of possessions and millions in the bank. My individual definition of success is centred around how I feel. Let me try and explain.

Rather than conform to the 'norm' of what success is perceived to be, or to live up to somebody else's definition of success, over the past 20 years or so I've set myself some targets to hit that have helped me to feel successful in my life. They have included:

- Getting out of bed
- Not giving up
- Stepping out of my comfort zone, if only for a second
- Speaking up and having my voice heard
- Enjoying my family
- Having friendships
- Laughing on a daily basis
- Feeling happy (see above)

- Trying something new
- Having enough
- Feeling good enough
- Offering value
- Feeling valued
- Being loved
- Loving others
- Feeling comfortable being 'me'.

You can see from this list that money and 'traditional' achievements don't feature in my definition of success. Instead, I've gone for things that help me to live a life on my terms. I've learned that the way I feel and the way I make others feel is a far better measure of success for me.

A good example of this is when I was looking for paid work again after deciding that self-employment wasn't for me. I didn't know what I wanted to do, but I knew how I wanted to feel. Job title and status mean nothing to me, but being able to be myself, to feel valued, and have fun means a lot. And the role I'm in at the moment offers me all I need to feel successful at work. And in my home life, I have everything I need to feel successful there too. But if I'd continued to believe my younger version's definition of success, it would be a very different story and I may never have had the opportunity to feel fulfilled and successful.

We need to start to create our own truths and keep reminding ourselves of them. Let's stop listening to what others tell us is happiness or success, because in my experience this only leads to frustration. Ensure you take the time to define what they actually mean to you, decide how you will measure them, and monitor your progress, celebrating the tiniest wins along the way. I've discovered that not comparing myself to others, and defining what success and happiness means to me is the only way for me to truly live a life on my terms.

What version of 'success' are you working towards, and how helpful is it?

"If you're not gonna tell me the truth, then why start talking?" Gene Wilder

WABI-SABI

FIND PERFECTION IN THE IMPERFECT

ACCEPT THAT THINGS ARE NOT FOREVER

EMBRACE THINGS IN THEIR MOST NATURAL STATE

APPRECIATE THE FLEETING AND THE IMPERFECT

THINGS DON'T NEED TO BE PERFECT,
PERMANENT, OR COMPLETE TO BRING HAPPINESS

JAPAN

14. The Invisible Man

"It always starts with you." Tim Roberts

Throughout this book I've talked about various times when I've felt stuck in my life and how I've moved away from those feelings to create a life lived more on my terms. But please don't take this as me being completely free of those feelings of not being good enough, or worrying about being 'found out', and of feeling stuck on occasions now.

Take this week for example (the third week in October 2022). When my alarm went off at 6am on Monday morning I just wasn't feeling 'it'. My wife had booked us a two-night break in the countryside over the weekend, so we spent Friday and Saturday in a lovely riverside hotel, enjoying walks, good food and the odd drink too many. And when I woke up, as much as I like my job, I just didn't want to go to work. I'd got a few things in my diary that I wasn't completely sure about. I won't bore you with the details but I was going to be delivering some face-to-face workshops and my fear of not being good enough was going into overdrive. One of these sessions was scheduled for this week so I was starting to feel the pressure. I'm not a perfectionist but I never want to look like a dick, and more importantly than that, I want to ensure that every session I deliver offers as much value as possible to the people on the session. Those who come to the workshops that I facilitate are expecting to learn something new and be able to walk away with different ways of thinking and ideas that they can action; and I was worried that I wouldn't be good enough for them.

It was dark and cold when I got out of bed and I felt like just dipping back under the duvet, giving up the salary, and living in a hut on a beach somewhere warm. It's not the first time I've felt like this; in fact, it's been a constant in my life. It goes back to that 'running away' thing. Maybe if I'd actually run away from home as a teenager, I'd have got it out of my system. Who knows? I'll certainly never know so there's no point lingering on that particular thought; I've realised that there's no point going over ifs, buts and maybes. If we are serious about taking control of our emotions and living a life that is built on being completely true to ourselves, we must deal in reality. We must seek out the truth of situations and work with facts. And the facts on that chilly Monday morning in October were that I was doubting my ability to deliver on what I was being paid to do. But where did those thoughts come from, and how had they managed to stick in my psyche?

I've received so much positive feedback over the last few years, I've been called inspirational and a joy to be around, with some people being kind enough to go public with their comments and sharing their thoughts on LinkedIn for the world to see.

"Steve is one of the friendliest and most inspirational people you could hope to work with" Ele George

"He is one of the most genuine people I have ever met professionally. He was a pleasure to work with and I, plus other colleagues hold his coaching, training, and presentation skills in high regard." Maureen Pascal

"Steve is an absolute joy to be around. He is positive, engaging, solution-focused and hugely productive. He is a wonderfully warm human being with a natural coaching ability." Kelly Joynes

These are just three examples of the kind of positive comments I receive, and from these it's obvious that I have an impact on those around me. So why do I still struggle at times to feel like I'm good enough? I've heard loads of inspirational speakers talk about the importance of creating a 'brag file' or the equivalent. In other words, keeping a note of all of the positive things that people say about you to refer to when you're lacking in confidence or if you need a reminder of what you've achieved and are in need of a little boost. This works to a certain extent for me, although usually on a relatively short-term basis. There's no denying that reading positive comments about yourself definitely helps you to think that you're doing something right, but what happens when it doesn't work; when it's not enough; when you stop believing what others are saying about you? Where do you go when the feelings of worthlessness and uselessness you have are so deep-rooted that no number of good reviews or positive comments make the slightest jot of difference?

I've discovered that this is where it is so important to know what you are all about, who you are, what is important to you, and why you are here. In other words, what is your purpose? My emotions have driven much of my life. I've lived a long time in the shadow of my past, and I've come to realise that I'm never going to escape what has happened to me. Unless I have a brain transplant my memories will always be there; and the feelings that they evoke will always have some power over the way that I think about myself, the behaviours I display, and the actions that I take. If I allow them to.

My past (all aspects of it) has brought me to this moment in time and the things that I've experienced have shaped me, but they don't have to define me. Trying to run away from my emotions hasn't worked. They always seem to find me regardless of where I am, who I'm with or what I'm doing; so I've decided to embrace how I feel. Whenever I'm not feeling the best, instead of brushing it under the carpet I 'sit' with the emotion. Whether it be anger, sadness, frustration, or loneliness I try to understand where it is coming from, what has triggered me to feel that way, and what the root cause might be.

For example, I regularly take Obi for a walk along the canal in the mornings. I love the peace and tranquillity of the tow-path. I often get to see a swan or two gliding gracefully, and a heron stalking the quiet waters. There are jays, ducks and moorhens that bring me joy, if I'm lucky I hear woodpeckers tapping away and I even see the odd bright blue kingfisher skimming across the surface of the water. And there are a couple of spots where, on clear mornings, the sunshine bursts through the trees and bathes the path in a warm glow and whenever I have the chance, I take a few minutes to bask in the morning heat. Eyes closed, I take a few deep breaths and listen to the wildlife around me. I lose myself in those moments and I absolutely love it. Nothing else matters; and even Obi has learned to stand calmly by my side whilst I enjoy the peace; something to be massively grateful for in itself as he is particularly high maintenance (in a really good way).

I share that stretch of canal with fellow walkers and a number of cyclists; and it's some of the cyclists' behaviour that I'd like to use to illustrate a point. Most cyclists are considerate; they slow down, say good morning, some even stop for us. But there are a number who never break a beat on their pedalling; they keep their heads down and ride towards us as if we don't exist. And there are those who ride up behind us, ringing their bell for us to get out of their way, seemingly with no consideration of how this makes us both jump. This makes me so angry and for the last two years or so since we've had Obi, I've been getting angrier and angrier at this behaviour. I've never confronted anybody but whenever I hear a bell ring, or see a cyclist hurtling towards me, my stomach tightens, and I feel my anger rising; usually culminating with me cursing under my breath as they whizz past me.

This feeling of anger has been bothering me for a while; it's beginning to spoil my enjoyment of the canal, and the thought of feeling angry has even stopped me from taking that route on occasions. Given the right circumstances I've always had a quick temper and getting angry has been part of 'who I am' for a very long time; but that's not how I want to feel. Having done so much work on myself over the past few years I recognise that these emotions are not who I am at all. The anger comes from somewhere deep inside me but, until recently, I've never taken the time to understand exactly where, and why. So I decided that rather than just accept that cyclists not slowing down on the canal made me angry, I would dig deeper into my thinking to discover where it comes from. I've worked out over the years that once I discover the root cause of my emotions, I'm much better placed to be able to do something about them and, as Mrs Nestor would say, "Choose to experience it in a different way."

It took quite a few walks along the canal, sitting with the feelings of anger whenever I was approached by a speeding cyclist before it started to become clear to me what my problem with the situation was. At first I thought it was simply that the cyclists weren't following the rules. I'd seen a sign on a different stretch of the canal that said that cyclists must give way to pedestrians, but when I worked that through I realised that I wasn't that bothered about people breaking the rules in such a minor way, so it must be something else. I thought that it could be the arrogance of the cyclists that was making me angry; expecting me to move out of their way simply because they were going faster than me. How would they like it if we were on the road and I sped towards them or drove up behind them in my car and beeped my horn so they'd move out of my way? But that wasn't it either. I'm not keen on arrogance, but I've learned to accept that some people just think they're better than everyone else and that the world owes them something, and regardless of who or what is in their way they're 'coming through.'

It wasn't either of these things, in fact I've realised that it has very little to do with canals or cyclists at all. My feelings of anger actually boiled down to me. For a long time in my life I felt invisible. I felt like nobody actually saw my face and I was always surprised when somebody I'd met remembered me. I never thought my voice was heard, so I had a tendency to not speak up and share my thoughts, ideas and feelings.

I thought that I'd dealt with this as over the last few years I've put myself out there by public speaking, delivering training, and facilitating workshops. I no longer feel invisible in my professional life and I'm quite happy being 'front and centre' with all eyes on me. I've mentioned before that there are pivotal moments in our lives that, if we allow them to, can influence our thinking and help us to see that there is a different way, and point us in a new direction. One of these moments for me was when I heard Emeli Sandé sing 'Read all about it (Part III)'[12] on the 12 August as part of the 2012 Summer Olympics closing ceremony. The lyrics in that song struck a chord deep within me immediately, and it has grown to be one of my favourite songs of all time. When I heard her singing about coming out from the shadows and sharing our voices it felt like she was directing her words at me and in that moment I knew that I had so much to offer but I had been terrified of stepping forward. Tracy and I had been together for around 10 years at that point and my confidence was growing but I still had huge doubts about myself and the way the world saw me. But I was starting to realise that my past didn't have to define me and that, with work, I could live the kind of life that I wanted to. Why shouldn't I use my voice? Why should I be scared of what people think?

And over the coming weeks and months I started to think differently. Another seed had been planted within me and I was determined to do all that I could to help it to take root and grow. I gradually started taking more control of my emotions and started to believe in myself. With Tracy's encouragement I'd started studying part-time for a degree with the Open University around three years earlier. Initially I'd signed up to do a Criminology degree with Psychological studies but after a couple of years realised that it wasn't for me so switched to an Open degree which allowed me to choose a variety of subjects to make up the credits needed for me to gain my qualification. This suited me as I wasn't studying for anything other than to prove to myself that I could do it.

I'd left school in 1987 with just two 'O' Levels (yes, I am that old. I was in the last year to do 'O' Levels). They were a grade C in Maths and a grade C in English Literature; confirming that I was thick! This was a belief that I held on to for a very long time, and whenever I was offered a job I was so grateful as I truly believed that I wasn't good enough for anything other than being used and beaten. I'm not sure if those around me at the time noticed how I felt about myself. I think I did a good job over the years of keeping my insecurities hidden but I've come to realise now that we just don't know what others see of us; we all have blind spots. Those behaviours, words and actions that others notice but we're unaware of. I wonder if anybody did see how unhappy I was; how lonely I felt; how useless and pointless I believed my life to be. Actually, it doesn't matter now; those days are long-gone and I'm a very different person as I write this today.

I'm so different in fact that I now know that if I'd been given the opportunity to focus on my studies instead of being made to satisfy his every need for most of my school life, I would have left school with far better qualifications as after six years of studying with the Open University, in 2015 I graduated with a First Class Honours Degree. During my six years I studied Crime, Welfare and Society, creative writing, religion and linguistics; and it was during my creative writing studies that I started to find my voice. Earlier in the book I gave a brief description of what happened to me in my childhood; this was an extract from a piece of life-writing that I produced as part of my studies and it was the first time that I'd written down anything about my experiences.

As part of the learning we had to critique one another's work during that year and I received some encouraging feedback on the way that I had told my story and had structured my writing, as well as a fair deal of sympathy for what I had been through from my fellow students and my tutor at the time. I went on to share this piece of writing in a blog that I created online, showing some of the people that I worked with at the time. I remember sharing my experiences with my manager who broke down in tears during my one-to-one. This has stuck with me ever since and has made me mindful of where and when to share my experiences. As my confidence and resilience has grown, and I've realised that I have nothing to be ashamed of because of what happened to me, it's become much easier to share my story. But I do feel that I have a responsibility to those around me to only share what is appropriate as I never want anybody to be 'triggered' or to feel uncomfortable by what I say. And this is one of the driving forces behind me wanting to write this book.

The example of my anger towards the cyclists on the tow-path just shows that although I've worked hard to feel the way that I want to feel I, like all of us, am still very much a work in progress. And it's so important to me that this message is heard loud and clear by all who read this book. Those deep-rooted beliefs of feeling worthless and invisible haven't completely disappeared; in fact they are still very much alive and kicking. By sitting with my anger and trying to understand where it comes from, rather than just accepting it as 'who I am' I realised that whenever a cyclist didn't slow down for me, the stories that I'd believed for so long were being subconsciously retold to me. But without taking the time and effort to think it through and to challenge my thinking, I never would have realised just how much I was still being governed by those thoughts. Leaving them unchecked and unchallenged for so long (it's not just cyclists on the tow-path I've felt this way about) has caused me to believe that I am just an angry man on so many occasions; when in fact, my anger isn't who I am, it is an emotion that I can control. And now I know the root cause of why I feel this way, I can put a plan in place to combat this feeling.

I did feel invisible for a long time; and when I think about it, I was invisible to many people. My pain was invisible to my friends and family. My bruises were invisible to those around me. The abuse I suffered was invisible to everybody outside of my home. My sadness and loneliness was invisible to the world. But none of that is the fault of the cyclists on the canal. And coming to this realisation has helped me to 'Choose to experience it in a different way.' Now when a cyclist comes towards me at full speed, I simply stop and let them pass. Rather than getting angry, I now reframe the story in my head. I imagine different scenarios that make it acceptable for them to be acting the way they are which helps me to feel calm and relaxed about the situation that, not so long along, made me angry. I tell myself that they must be in a rush. Maybe they're late for work? Maybe they have a big family and have to get the children ready before leaving? Maybe they've just finished work and are rushing home to look after someone who relies on them? Realising that my anger came from the thought that I was invisible to them, helped me to question that deep-rooted feeling; especially the anger caused by the bell-ringing brigade. If I truly was invisible to them, why would they even bother ringing their bell?

We're constantly telling ourselves stories, and they're not always the most helpful. I have allowed myself to feel angry at those cyclists on the canal for too long and the only person who has suffered is me. They don't know how I was feeling as they rode past me but I let it eat away at me, and I was even in danger of allowing my feelings to jeopardise a simple pleasure of mine. By focusing on the way we feel, accepting that we are not our emotions, and realising that when we understand why we feel a particular way, we give ourselves the power to move towards living a life on our own terms. This example might seem a little trivial, but believe me, it has made such a difference to my life. Recognising that just because I had one aspect of my life under control, didn't mean that all of my life was in the same place was massive and makes me realise that regardless of what others see on the surface, I have to constantly battle with the story-teller within me that seems desperate to pull me back to a place that I thought I'd escaped.

It's important for me to share this as there are too many people out there who are struggling for many different reasons. I want to show that regardless of where you are, you should never compare yourself to anybody but you. It's good to have role models, people whose behaviours we can take positives from, but we always have to remember that we only ever see what people want us to see and we have to be careful to not believe that everybody around us is doing better than us. As I said earlier in the book, I'm a middle-aged man who has experienced my fair share of challenges and have come through the other side and found my own version of happiness, success and contentment, but that's not the end of the story. It's a constant battle to stay on track, but with commitment and a vision for how I want to feel, I can keep going in the right direction. And my hope is that my experiences can help you to do the same thing.

Having a vision of how I want to feel has been my saviour on so many occasions over the last few years. Going back to my worries that I mentioned earlier in this chapter, there were two instances in particular that were on my mind when I was considering running off to live on a desert island. Without going into too much detail, I design and facilitate learning experiences covering leadership, management, coaching, and Equality, Diversity & Inclusion and I was due to deliver a couple of face-to-face sessions that were taking up a lot of my thoughts, and not in a particularly positive way.

As confident as I am that I can deliver great sessions and help people to feel 'safe' and to empower them to have the conversations and ask the questions that will really bring their learning to life, I still have huge doubts whenever I'm about to facilitate any session (online or face-to-face). The responsibility that I feel and the pressure I put myself under will always be there. I sometimes struggle to understand what value I can actually bring, which leads to a crisis of confidence and a temptation to hide under the covers, especially on cold, dark Monday mornings.

On both of the occasions in question, I got myself into a bit of a mini-state, allowing the old stories to take centre-stage in my mind. I'm thick so what could they possibly take from spending time with. I'm useless, so I was bound to mess up at some point, so why bother even trying. I'm worthless and pointless; if only they knew what a waste of space I was, they'd never want me anywhere near their development programmes. These thoughts began to manifest themselves in my actions and behaviours. My mood changed and I felt myself becoming irritable. Thankfully it wasn't for long as I've learned to spot the triggers and signs that have previously taken me into a spiral of self-pity but it was for long enough for me to realise that I will always have something to contend with; the remnants of my past are like parasites inside my mind. They feed on the slightest insecurity and, if they remained unchallenged, they could grow into something far bigger and more powerful than they ever should be. My logical brain tells me that these thoughts are untrue, that there is no evidence to support them; in fact, there's loads of evidence to support the exact opposite. But logic and perspective go out of the window when we allow our 'unthinking' brain to take over.

You know the one I'm talking about. The brain that believes all the shit it's been fed over the years, the brain that doesn't question the negative self-talk, the brain that ignores all the good stuff and puts all the bad stuff centre-stage in the glare of the brightest spotlight. The brain that quite likes being the victim in a funny sort of way as it devolves us of all responsibility for ourselves.

The way I've learned to overcome this unhelpful kind of thinking is to shift my energy. There is always a different way to see things, and sometimes it's the slightest shifts that make the biggest difference. Sometimes it's simply changing position that can help. I've found that when I consciously move from a spot where my mood is not the most positive, I have developed the ability to be able to see whatever challenges I have in that moment from a different perspective. And once I've seen them from another angle, I gain hope that I can overcome them, or at least change the way I feel about them. I choose my words deliberately here when I say 'developed the ability' because that is what I've done. I've taken the time to recognise when something needs to change and I've tried various strategies and techniques until I've found the ones that work for me. And what works for me is pretty straightforward. I like to keep things as simple as possible!

When I'm feeling down or stuck I shift my physical energy. In other words, if I'm sitting at my desk in front of my laptop, I go into the kitchen and put some music on, or into the garden, or for a walk, or pick up a book, or do some drawing. I question why I feel the way I do. Am I bored? (which is often the case). Am I upset? Am I angry? Am I frustrated? Am I tired? Hungry? Is something else happening in my life that's affecting my thought process?

Our energy flows where our attention goes. In other words if we continue to focus on the things that make us feel upset, angry, bored, or frustrated then there's a pretty good chance we'll continue to feel that way. So once I've sat with the 'negative' emotion for a while, and have looked at it from different perspectives to understand where it's coming from I can start to think how I'd like to feel instead, and begin to focus my attention on the positive. And this is what I did when I was worried about the two sessions I've been referring to throughout this chapter.

"How are your assumptions influencing your thoughts and behaviours?"

I realised that I was worried because I was putting too much emphasis on how I hoped the delegates would feel during the sessions. My assumptions about their expectations were leading me to believe that they would be hoping to walk away with a wealth of new, exciting knowledge that would help them to be the next top business leaders. The more I sat at my laptop looking at the content for the session, the more negative stories I told myself. And once I realised that the laptop was the 'trigger' for my emotions I decided to go back to basics. I took a blank piece of paper and a few colourful pens and sat at the breakfast bar with Guns 'n' Roses blasting out across the kitchen. Instead of worrying about the things I can't control, namely how the delegates would feel about the sessions, and the amount of learning they would take from them, I focused on how I'd like to feel at the end of the sessions instead.

What would success feel like for me? And after a few minutes I realised that I didn't need the colourful pens. I quickly came to the conclusion that success for me would come in the form of the reaction from the delegates to my style of delivery. If I could get them engaged, talking, laughing, sharing stories, thoughts, and ideas, that would be my measure of success. And I knew that I could do that so I was on to a winner straight away. I'd spent so long being hung up on the details of the programme and thinking about things that I had no control over that I'd almost become paralysed. But recognising my negative emotions and simply shifting my position and taking a different approach helped me to refocus and ultimately deliver two sessions that I absolutely loved facilitating, and the delegates found valuable, enjoyable and insightful. And when asked to describe (in no more than two words) how they felt at the end of the sessions, they said;

- Challenged
- Inspired
- Thought-provoked
- Valued
- Reflective
- Empowered
- Intrigued
- Eyes-opened
- Determined
- Comfortably uncomfortable.

I don't think it gets much better than that and just shows what an impact we can have when we focus on what we can control. When we decide how we want to feel, and when we take the time and effort to define what success means to us as individuals, we can challenge those unhelpful stories and the assumptions we make, and we can overcome our fears.

"If I'd only understood how possible it was to become unstuck and that the power to feel positive, resilient, and confident lay in my hands all along I would have taken the steps I have much sooner."

Steve Nestor

15. Give a little respect (to yourself)

"If nothing changes, nothing changes."
Joe Fallone

In the summer of 2022 I was lucky enough to be asked to travel to Sydney for work. It was all a bit last minute and a touch surreal. It was only a matter of weeks from being asked if I'd like to go, to stepping off the plane on the other side of the world. I'd never been to Australia before and couldn't believe that I was being given this opportunity. My trip would include three days of work, spending four nights outside the city, and a day or so of free time either side to explore Sydney. I was only going for a week but that wasn't a problem as I was flying Business Class; another first for me. I was on such a high. How lucky was I?

But remember that I told you earlier in the book that my dad died of a heart attack at the age of 51 when he had gone back to Australia. Well, I was 51 when I visited Sydney, and as I was taking in the iconic landmarks as we came into land, I had to fight with my inner storyteller that was desperate to convince me that fate (even though I'm not sure I believe in it) had brought me to the Land Down Under to end my days on this earth. Luckily it was only a relatively fleeting thought as I've worked hard over the years to ensure that I can step away from unhelpful and disempowering thoughts as they have held me back for far too long. By challenging the validity of my thinking and sense checking the facts against the assumptions, I managed to pull excitement and positivity back to the front of my mind, enabling me to take in and enjoy the potential once-in-a-lifetime experience.

The trip went brilliantly, with the added bonus of me not dying. Work was great and I managed to cram in loads of sightseeing whilst in the city. I watched the sun rise over Sydney Harbour Bridge, took a ferry to Manly and walked along the beautiful beach, watched seals playing in the shadow of the famous Opera House, and savoured delicious meals in Barangaroo and Darling Harbour. The flights and Business Class lounges were amazing. Experiencing how the other half live was incredible. Having my own pod with TV and fully reclining chair that doubled as a bed; having drinks of my choice on tap and top restaurant quality food served on proper plates ensured that the journey literally flew by. Imagine if throwing myself down the stairs when I was a young teenager had resulted in a different outcome. I would never have had the opportunity to have this amazing experience.

I was away from home for nine nights in total and although I loved my time in Australia I missed my wife. I've realised that the joy of experiencing things for me lies in sharing. I'm more than happy in my own company. I like being in control of what I do and where I go, and I love exploring and meeting new people. But my wife is my best friend. She is always there for me, and has been so supportive since the moment we met, and I would have loved nothing more than to explore Sydney for the first time with her. But the reason for sharing this experience has little to do with what actually happened whilst I was travelling, or my feelings of how I'd have loved my wife to be with me. It's actually about parking. Let me explain.

All of my expenses, as you'd expect, were covered by the company so why did I choose to park my car miles from Heathrow airport in a dodgy, dusty car park? Why did I decide to go for the cheapest option? The one where I had to wait for a rickety minibus to collect me from the airport for the 25-minute drive back to my car. The option where I had to wait for nearly an hour for that minibus to collect me from Heathrow after my 30-hour journey from the other side of the world. The option that saw me squashed against the window of a packed mini-bus with the hairy legs of an ex-rugby player rubbing against me.

I'll tell you why. It's because regardless of how much work I've done on myself over the last few years, fundamentally I still have very little respect for myself. This lack of self-worth led me to book the cheapest parking I could find, in spite of knowing that this certainly wouldn't be what was expected of me. This lack of respect for myself led me to believe that I wasn't worth the little extra money it would cost to park within walking distance of the arrivals terminal.

Talking this through with Tracy over a couple of drinks recently made me realise that I still don't feel worthy. During that conversation Tracy told me how angry it makes her at times that I still obviously think so little of myself. It frustrates and upsets her because she sees me in a totally different light (she always has). She told me that if she'd known I was booking that parking she would have challenged my thinking and convinced me to go for the more convenient option.

This lack of self-worth has manifested itself in so many different ways over the years and this latest realisation confirms that I still have work to do and this is a further demonstration that I am very much a work in progress. As I've said throughout this book, I believe that we can learn from every experience that we go through and move towards living a life on our terms if we take the time to reflect, to understand what drives our behaviours, to believe that it doesn't always have to be this way, and to be willing to put the work in to change and grow.

And what I've learned following my trip to Australia is that I need to learn how to respect myself more. I've come a long way, but if I'm to fully reach my own potential, there's more work to be done. And that work starts now. From this moment forward (1.52pm on Sunday 6 November 2022) I'm committing to never accepting less than I am worth. And that worth will not be determined by what others think of me, or how I'm treated by my peers, friends, colleagues, family, or strangers. My worth will be determined by me, and me alone.

But how am I going to do this? It's okay saying this stuff, but putting it into action and actually doing something about it is easier said than done. As I mentioned earlier, I've realised over the years that if I try to take on too many ideas or new actions at any one time I very often don't follow through on any of them, so I like to keep things as simple as possible. That's why I've committed to just one simple action to help me to build my self-worth.

Whenever I'm about to make a decision; whether it's on airport parking, choice of meal in a restaurant, a new pair of shoes, or absolutely anything else in life, I'm going to remind myself of how I felt whilst waiting for that minibus to arrive. How tired I was; how frustrated I felt when the driver told me that he was only five minutes away, when in fact it would be nearly an hour before he got to me; how it felt to be squashed up against the window of the jam-packed minibus on the journey back to the car park; how it felt to see my freshly cleaned car looking as though it had been parked in the Sahara Desert during a sandstorm; how it felt to have to wait another 20 minutes at the car park whilst the cars in front of mine were moved before beginning my two and half hour drive home; how much nicer it would have been to have arrived home to my wife before 9pm rather than just after 11pm. And I'm going to ask myself if the decision I'm about to take will make me feel as happy as I possibly can be.

Whilst writing this I'm reminded of something that my father-in-law, Les, once said. He was sharing some of his many life experiences and was talking about how it's important to enjoy all that life has to offer and to ensure that whenever possible, to take the opportunities that are presented to you. He said "Never push your nose up against the window," and I'm now ready to take this piece of advice and run with it. Never again will I disrespect myself. From now on there'll be no more 'pushing my nose up against the window', no more settling for second best, or taking the cheapest option. I'll be taking a seat at the top table and choosing the options that are best for me. Not because I'm arrogant or think that I'm better than anyone else, but because

I've spent my whole life compromising and not valuing and respecting myself and that has got to change.

I started writing this book because I have a story to share that I hope will encourage others to believe in themselves, and during the writing of it I'm continuing to find out more about myself every single day. Self-awareness is a never-ending process, and questioning our actions and behaviours in a bid to understanding what is driving us is crucial to being able to move forward and feel happy, content, and comfortable in our own skin ... and I sincerely hope that my words and experiences are helping you to become the best version of you that you possibly can be.

16. Different faces for different places

"Courage is being scared to death, but saddling up anyway." John Wayne

I've spent a lot of my life living in the shadows. I've stayed out of the spotlight, I've held back and not been myself. As I've mentioned, I felt invisible for a long time and got used to believing that nobody could see me. It was a safe place where I could be me without fear of being ridiculed for not fitting in, for not thinking in the same way as others, for being content with not being 'one of the lads.'

I don't suppose I'm alone in this but for years I've 'pretended' to be different people depending on where I am. We all have different faces for different places, we are human beings and act in different ways depending on where we are, what we're doing and who we're with. For example it wouldn't feel appropriate to bring my 'watching football' face or my 'getting on my political soapbox' face to a meeting at work. In the same way that I don't wear my 'meeting with a client' face on a night out with friends.

This 'switching of hats' is something I feel I've (we've) been conditioned to do. To fit the norms of convention we have to act in a particular way when we're in a certain setting. But who says? Who says that I shouldn't share my political views with a group of people I'm working with? Who says I shouldn't talk about what upsets me with a new client? Who says that I shouldn't be me in every place that I find myself? The answer is that nobody has ever said that I shouldn't be me. Nobody but me. And over the last few years I've started to find my voice and become more confident to be myself wherever I am.

How often do you bend to fit into the 'norms' of the situations you find yourself in? How often do you bite your tongue when you want to share your views? How often do you feel that because everyone is sharing their ideas you have to say something, even though you may naturally be someone who likes to reflect before sharing your thoughts? Regardless of whether you want to speak up and don't, or are made to feel that you should speak up when you don't want to, you are not allowing yourself to be you.

What a shame it is that many of us go through life not being our true selves. I've realised from my own experiences that often the only reason I wasn't always true to myself was that I allowed my assumptions to influence my actions, words and behaviours.

- I assumed that nobody would want to hear my thoughts and ideas
- I assumed that being myself would make me look weak
- I assumed that people wouldn't take me seriously if I shared my emotions and vulnerabilities.

I've come to realise that rather than continue to struggle to fit into the so-called 'norms' of life, to live a life on my terms, I need to take a chance and just start being me. And what a difference it's making. Being me is what I'm best at so why have I been hiding it away for so long?

Lack of confidence and self-worth, and believing the stories and negative self-talk have all been contributing factors but society might not have helped either. As well as the abuse, I grew up in a time when 'children should be seen and not heard,' and at school we were threatened with the cane across the backside or the ruler across our knuckles if we spoke out or questioned anything. Couple this with the constant threat of a beating (or worse) at home if I ever dared to challenge or speak without being spoken to and it's hardly any surprise that I (along with many others) struggle to trust that we can share our thoughts without retribution or judgement being passed on us, and that we do have a voice worth listening to. But just because that's how it was, doesn't mean that is how it should always be.

I've realised that most of this learned behaviour of not being comfortable with being who I am comes from a lack of confidence and that old foe of mine; the feeling of worthlessness. Reflecting on my behaviour over the years I've noticed a few patterns that have contributed to reinforcing these negative feelings, one of the major ones was my inability to accept compliments.

My view of the world, and all the things that people say to me, is filtered by my experiences, my thoughts, my assumptions, and the stories I've been told and continue to tell myself. And the majority of those filters block anything positive from entering my mind because that doesn't fit with my view of my world. So any compliment that I ever received was batted off because I didn't believe for a second that anybody could possibly see anything good in me, or about me. Looking back I can hear myself saying things like; 'I was lucky' when I hit my targets at work or was offered a promotion, and 'I've had this ages, it was dead cheap' when I was complimented on a new shirt I'd bought.

The filters that told me that I wasn't worthy didn't allow me to see that people were interested in me, that they valued me, that they could see what I wasn't allowing myself to see; that I was good at what I did and that I could look nice. And not because they wanted anything from me, they were just being truthful and kind.

Learning to take compliments and to stop batting them off has been one the most important lessons in helping to build my confidence and improving my feelings of self-worth. Simply saying 'thank you' when somebody complimented me helped me to begin to question the filters which I'd always seen the world through and allowed a little bit of positivity to seep into my psyche. I say 'simply saying thank you' but it's not as easy as it sounds when you don't value yourself, and it takes practice to get into the habit of accepting that you are not always how you think about yourself.

It may feel uncomfortable hearing something positive about yourself (it certainly was for me) so getting used to feeling uncomfortably comfortable is crucial. Even though every fibre inside me was screaming to push away any compliment I received I slowly learned to just say thank you. On reflection, it was a bit robotic at first. I'd say thank you and quickly move on, changing the subject and shifting the attention away from me. But over time it became easier, less uncomfortable and I actually started to believe what they were saying. Practice makes perfect, and forming new habits and thinking patterns takes time, and now I accept compliments easily because I know that I deserve them. Whether it be for work that I've done, the way that I look, or how I've made someone feel, I've learned to accept that the way people see me is a true reflection of who I am and the positive impact I have on those around me.

"We need to be comfortably uncomfortable" Nicole Foster

The key message here is that we can learn new ways of thinking, and once I realised this, and started to feel 'uncomfortably comfortable' when people were saying nice things to me. My mindset, slowly but surely, shifted from one of pure negativity towards myself, to one of possibility. If people around me could see good in me, maybe, just maybe I wasn't bad after all. And once I started to think this way, it was a small step to start thinking that maybe I was actually good and worthy of praise. I can't underestimate the power of feeling valued and worthy of praise. We believe the stories we tell ourselves and if those stories include the belief that we have qualities that others appreciate, then we might just start to value ourselves.

17. Grow; Into the very best version of you

"You can't get a suit of armour and a rubber chicken just like that. You have to plan ahead." Michael Palin

The first time I went to Greece on holiday and I told the coach driver my surname I was a little taken aback by his response. He went from a bored looking middle-aged chap slouched behind the steering wheel, to an animated, twinkly eyed, excited 'schoolboy'. I didn't understand the fuss and was a touch confused by his reaction so as soon as we got to the hotel I Googled Nestor.

It turns out that in Greek Mythology, Nestor[13] was the King of Pylos. He was an Argonaut and helped Jason to retrieve the Golden Fleece. He was distinguished as a warrior, and was also known for his potentially overwhelming hospitality, he was a wise ruler who was always called on for advice. Nestor's most striking features are said to be his wisdom, justice, bravery, knowledge of war, and his eloquence.

The coach driver's reaction and my research helped me to see myself in a different light and has given me another way to describe myself. Although it is Greek Mythology, Nestor, King of Pylos has now become part of my story, part of who I am, and if nothing else, acts as a good conversation starter.

The reason for sharing this is to show that we can describe ourselves in many different ways. This can help us to take a step back from our reality and see things from a different perspective. And looking at myself from various angles (real or mythological) has helped me to think about things differently.

There have been times when I've felt stuck or nervous about something and I've imagined what the King of Pylos would do in that situation, and I've then channelled my inner 'Nestor' and tried something new or stepped out of my comfort zone. One example of this was when I was asked to speak at a National Conference on the power of storytelling. As the day approached I was feeling a bit apprehensive about it to say the least, so I imagined how the eloquent King of Pylos might approach it, and whether he would be nervous about speaking in front of over 100 people. I came to the conclusion that rather than be nervous, Nestor would relish the chance to have his voice heard, which helped me to embrace the opportunity and make the most of it. If he could enjoy it, why shouldn't I? And although I was still nervous when I began to speak, I soon settled down and delivered an inspirational talk that received high praise, adding another notch of confidence and creating a reference point for me to reflect on and learn from whenever I've found myself in similar situations since.

Growth, progression and living a life on your terms is possible for every single one of us, but it doesn't happen without planning, setting goals, and putting the work in. Not many of us get handed things on a plate but once we start to realise that we are as important as every other person in this world, we become motivated to take the actions that will move us forward.

Before I met Tracy there was no way in this world that I thought I'd study for a degree. I never dreamt that I'd be a public speaker, that I'd have a career in learning and development, or that I'd write a book. But more important than all of those things, I never thought that I was worthy of a decent life. But slowly and surely I started to believe the things that she was telling me and I started to try things out, to put myself out there little by little. Rather than hide away and say 'no' to things, I began to step forward more and more. Even when I was terrified inside (and I still get those feelings), I pushed on, and the more I did, the more confident I became; and the more confident I became, the more I did.

As I said at the beginning of this book, I'm not a millionaire, or an inspirational sports star with a 'secret' formula for success. I'm a 'just' a man who has been through some stuff and I've decided to tell my story in the hope that it brings value to your life; in the hope that if you're feeling stuck or in need of a little kindness at this moment in time it gives you the belief that things won't always be this way for you.

Lessons from the Cowboy Code

Seeing as I've called this book Reflections of a Cowboy it seems only right to share the ten principles of Code of the West as listed on CowboyEthics.org[2] with a few sentences on how I interpret the headlines to help me to live a life on my terms. Just to be clear, I've never read the Cowboy Ethics book, I just used the headings on the website and interpreted them in a way that works for me so any similarities will be purely coincidental. Please feel free to add your own interpretations if you find that helpful.

1. Live each day with courage

Be brave and put yourself out there. If you feel that something needs to change, take action and make it happen. Challenge yourself and step out of your comfort zone.

2. Take pride in your work

If you're in, make sure you give 100%. Prepare well, work hard, and believe that you can make a difference in whatever you're doing. And take pride in yourself, celebrate your achievements and what you stand for.

3. Always finish what you start

Unless you realise that it's not what you want or need in your life. Things change so always remember to be kind yourself. If something is not serving you well, stop doing it. But once you're clear on what you want and why it is important to you, keep going, stick with it and trust in the process.

4. Do what has to be done

Do whatever you have to do to understand yourself, to discover your purpose, to define what happiness, success and living a life on your terms means for you. And commit to taking the actions that will help you to get closer to where you want to be.

5. Be tough, but fair

For me, this is all about making those tough decisions and answering those tough questions about yourself that you may have been avoiding. It's easy to shy away from things and stay in our comfort zone but will that always get you the life you want? This is also about being fair (and kind) to yourself.

6. When you make a promise, keep it

Whether it's a promise to yourself, or somebody else, do what you say you will, and be consistent. In my experience, carrying out my commitments has led to me forming stronger relationships that have helped to increase my confidence, resilience and happiness.

7. Ride for the brand

It's all about you. Be true to yourself. Learn what's important to you and work towards living a life on your terms. Be clear on what your purpose is and consider what legacy you would like to leave. Don't be afraid to show the world who you are and what you're all about.

8. Talk less and say more

Actions speak louder than words. Know your worth, know your purpose and show the world how important you are. Don't get stuck talking about the things you want and need in your life, take action; and give the world something positive to say about you.

9. Remember that some things aren't for sale

What are your values? What are your non-negotiables?

Develop your self- awareness and never compromise on the things that you hold dear to your heart.

10. Know where to draw the line

How will you know when enough is more than enough? How will you know when you are enough? What do you need to say 'no' to? Remember, if you're saying 'yes' to this, what are you saying 'no' to? How do you ensure that you are being kind to yourself?

"I've realsied that I stood in my own way for a very long time and it was only when I started thinking in terms of what I wanted and how I wanted to feel, that things started to change."

Steve Nestor

18. Ride for the brand

"It's all about people. We're all just people helping people, helping people."
Kira Burrows

There are so many stories that are entwined within mine. There is my sister's story, she is four years younger than me and grew up in the same household. There are the stories of my two eldest children Leah and Dan, whose mum and my first wife, Jenny, sadly died when she was just forty-years-old. There's Tracy's son's story. Jack was just 18 months old when I met his mum and has been part of my life ever since. There is our youngest son, Sam's story. There is my mum's story. And, of course, there is Tracy's story.

I've deliberately told this story from my point of view as that is the only way that I can do it. I did contemplate talking more about my children and Jenny's death and the impact that had on me and on us as a family but it didn't feel right to do so. I was massively impacted by Jenny's passing, I was shocked and deeply saddened. And still am when I think about how it must feel for my children, but that has nothing to do with why I'm writing this book. We all experience sadness and loss at some point in our lives and, as I've said throughout, we can choose to take the lessons from our pain to help us to move forward. But the lessons I learned from Jenny's death are not ones that I think I should be sharing on these pages. I simply wanted to mention her as she was a big part of my life for so long, and to let my children know how proud I am of them for the way they have handled everything that life has thrown at them to carve out happy and successful lives for themselves.

I've realised that I've spent my whole life running away; physically and emotionally. I've jumped from job-to-job, and from place-to-place. On reflection it was a case of getting away from where I was or how I was feeling, rather than making the move because I was desperate to do that new thing. I never thought about what I wanted, it was always about what I didn't want, and how to escape it. I always thought that if I could experience that new thing that everything would be okay. But that was never the case. And if I'm totally honest, although I'm in a much better place in my life now and am no longer physically running away from anything, I still have my ongoing challenges as I've shown throughout this book.

Another example of this is my inability to say 'no' to things, particularly in a work capacity. I've recently realised that even when I'm told that it's okay to say 'no', I really struggle with it. Recognising this in myself I've been trying to get to the root cause of why this might be by firstly watching out for the physiological triggers; in other words, how does my body react. I've learnt that whenever I'm asked to do anything or get involved in something my stomach instantly tightens. And when I think about saying 'no' it tightens even further and the only time it begins to loosen is when I say 'yes'. I've been reassured that saying 'no' to things is okay; and I've tried to embrace this but I find it really difficult. Even writing this down is making me feel uncomfortable. It's as if in my mind I'm showing some kind of weakness, some kind of inability to manage, or to cope with what I'm being asked to do.

But I know it runs deeper than that. When I've dug into the reasons why saying 'no' is such a problem for me I've realised that whenever in my past I've not agreed to do something, there has very often been a negative consequence for me. In childhood there were multiple occasions when he told me to lie still, or to open my mouth so he could get his pleasure and I protested and wriggled and clamped my mouth shut only to be punched in the gut or grabbed around the throat until I succumbed to his wishes. But there are also the more subtle examples; the times when I had to say no to going out to play so that he could spend the afternoon in bed with me, and the times when saying no to going to a school disco or party led to me feeling like I'd never have any friends and the deep sadness and feelings of loneliness that led to.

I've realised that I've always been afraid of saying 'no' but have never thought about why. And the reasons why clash with the stories that I've told myself. If you Google 'a fear of saying no' one thing that you'll find is that it often comes from the urge to avoid conflict. Over the years I've told myself (and others) that I'm 'happy' with conflict. I'm not bothered by a bit of a disagreement. Bring it on… physical or emotional, I'm ready for it and will happily stand my ground. What a load of crap!

I realise now that I've been terrified by conflict my whole life. Now that I think about it, whenever I hear an argument brewing, or see a fight starting my stomach starts doing somersaults and begins to tighten. Raised voices and disagreements really bother me; but I've always told myself that I'm okay with them. I was a bailiff for a while and I convinced myself that I revelled in the fact that some people were confrontational with me, but I realise now that the reality is that I hated every second of it.

As with many of the stories I've told myself over the years, this one of being okay with conflict has been constructed without me realising what I was doing. I was telling myself these things to protect myself. Maybe I wasn't ready to face the truth because admitting that I was scared of conflict might make me feel even weaker and more useless than I already did. Maybe I just wasn't ready to face the work I'd have to do that would be needed to create a whole new story for myself. A story where saying 'no' is easy because I'd know that nothing bad would come from it. As I write these words I realise that I am ready to write that new story now, but I understand that it won't happen overnight; and that's okay because we are all a continual work in progress. I've come a long way, but by no means am I (or suspect will ever be) the finished article. And realising that gives me the strength and determination to keep moving forward towards feeling the way that I want to feel on a more regular basis. Being honest with myself has been hard, and I'm sure I have a few more truths to uncover in my life, but taking the time to discover the root causes that lead to some of my behaviours has been so enlightening and is helping me to understand what I want in life and to work towards that positive feeling, rather than away from the negative.

For years I floated around not knowing where I was going or what was important to me. I've done so may jobs including apprentice sheet metal worker, croupier, sales executive, kitchen maker, security van driver, manager, bailiff, support worker, factory worker, order picker, marketing & communications specialist, Asda delivery driver, business owner, professional coach, facilitator, and learning & development consultant; often jumping without much thought from one to the next in the hope that it would bring me happiness and contentment.

The saying 'jumping out of the frying pan and into the fire' couldn't be truer when I think of some of the moves I've made, but do you know what, when I reflect on my colourful career, I've learned something new about myself every time I started something different. When I was working for myself as a coach, mentor and facilitator, I took a part-time job driving with Asda delivering groceries three evenings a week. This wasn't in my plan but was possibly one of the most important moves I've made. I had a few contracts as a coach that were helping me to make a living but as a new business owner I needed to earn a little extra whilst I was building my reputation and my client list. I really enjoyed that driving job and it was during those shifts where I was out on the road, working alone that I found the time and space to be able to think about what I actually wanted from my life. How I wanted to feel, and the impact I wanted to make on the world. It was during one of my breaks, sitting in the cab of my van in a layby, watching the sun set over the open farmer's fields opposite the layby that I was parked in that the idea of creating a cowboy style Wanted poster to 'sell' myself was born. I have lots of transferable skills that I've gathered along the way and I wasn't sure 'what' I wanted to be. But that time to reflect helped me to understand the things that are important to me. So I decided to tell the world who I was, what was important to me, what I could offer, and how I wanted to feel which led me to my current role as a Learning & Development Consultant.

Everything I've been through has brought me to this point in my life. If I'd stood still and waited for life to happen to me I'd possibly still be living a very miserable life where I believed that being invisible was the best place for me. I'd possibly still be held back by my belief that I was worthless, thick, and useless.

I've discovered over the years that it's important for me to have something bigger in my life that enables me to embrace all of my experiences, and the emotions they evoke, and to celebrate them for what they bring to my day to day. I've realised that we often push emotions to one side because we are not fully in control of them and are 'scared' of where they might take us. There have been times in my life that if I'd let myself cry, I feel that I would have ended up a blubbering wreck for days or weeks on end; or if I'd allowed myself to express my anger, I'd have probably ended up in the back of a police car; and how might that have affected my life choices and chances?

In those times I believed everything that was happening was totally out of my control, my emotions ruled me. I believed that I was just an angry person, a sad person, a person with no confidence who just had to 'suck it up' and live with being worthless. I felt like that for a very long time but since becoming a qualified coach, I've realised that I control my emotions and can decide how I'd like to respond in any given moment. I also discovered how important it is to have a purpose in life. Something that puts everything into perspective. A reason to get out of bed. Something that brings fulfilment to my life and helps me to flourish every single day.

I'm not religious. I suppose I could be described as 'spiritual' in so much as I believe there's a greater meaning to us being on this earth other than just being born, getting on the conveyor belt of school, work, pay your taxes, have the odd holiday (if you're lucky), retire, and then lie on our death-bed regretting all the things we didn't get to do before our lights go out for the last time.

After reading 'Man's search for meaning' by Viktor Frankl[14] where he talks about the importance of identifying a purpose in life to feel positive about, I realised that if he could get through some of the worst experiences imaginable during his time in Nazi concentration camps, then I needed to take a leaf out his book and find my purpose in life. His theory of Logotherapy is based on the belief that human nature is motivated by the search for a life of purpose. In other words, Logotherapy is the pursuit of the meaning of your life. And over the last few years I've been doing just that.

Like everything that's worth having, it takes time, effort, and commitment and is an ongoing process. In a world where people seem to be searching for quick wins for everything from losing weight to making their fortune, it's not always the easiest thing to be patient, to take the time to reflect and be willing to accept that we can learn from all of our experiences regardless of whether they're good, bad or ugly (do you like the cowboy film reference I squeezed in there).

Finding my meaning and purpose in life has been so important to me and has helped me to feel that I am actually contributing something valuable to the world. As I said earlier, this is an ongoing process, but thanks to taking the time to reflect and being really honest with myself I live my life by the very simple, three-word formula that I created when running my own consultancy business. Reflect, Believe, Grow. And working on this process helped me to realise that my purpose in life is to:

Stimulate reflection, inspire belief and ignite growth to enable myself and those around me to flourish.

WANTED

An engaging, challenging, and meaningful role that plays to my strengths, in an organisation that truly believes in the potential of people.

STEVE NESTOR

BA(Hons)First Class

GUILTY OF:

Qualified coach & mentor
People development
Team leadership
Clear communication
Project management
Prioritising wellbeing

GUILTY OF:

ILM Level 5 Coaching & Mentoring
Strengthscope practitioner
Emotional Intelligence practitioner
Mental Health First Aider
Believing in people
Creativity, collaboration & curiosity

APPROACH WITH A SMILE & AN OPEN MIND

Let's have a conversation and a few laughs around a campfire with a whisky or two
Mobile: 07918 754815
Email: stevenestor99@gmail.com

REWARD

Upon capture you'll receive a passionate, motivated professional with more than 30 years of comprehensive experience developing exceptional relationships with clients, peers, customers, colleagues, and senior leadership to provide sustainable business solutions.

Excellent people, performance, and personal management skills with key strengths in coaching, mentoring, training, communication and leadership.

Employing a growth mindset to solution finding, Steve's a dedicated, personable professional with the drive and skills to excel in any role. With the ability to effortlessly empower others to flourish and fulfil their individual potential, his experience and knowledge will enhance the ability of any organisation to create high performing teams, sustainable change, and a culture of continuous improvement.

Ikigai

Now we've touched on why I believe it's important to find your purpose, I'll explain how I began to discover mine. Triggered by reading Viktor Frankl's book, I went in search of what my purpose could be. Immersing myself in self-help books but feeling frustrated that nothing was hitting the mark for me, until I remembered a good friend of mine, Jo Mason, had once talked about Ikigai; the Japanese Secret to a Long and Happy Life[15]. So I jumped onto Amazon and ordered myself a copy. A few days later this gorgeous little light blue hardback book with a blossom branch on the front cover landed on my doorstep; and along with Matt Haig's Reasons to Stay Alive and Viktor Frankl's Man's Search for Meaning, that beautiful little book has been one of the most influential things I've ever read.

Ikigai, according to Hector Garcia and Francesc Mirales brilliant book, is 'The Japanese Secret to a Long and Happy Life.' Finding your Ikigai, 'a reason to jump out of bed every morning' involves exploring four stages;

- What you love
- What you're good at
- What the world needs
- What you can get paid for.

The theory goes that when you discover what you love and what you're good at, you will find your passion. Combining what you love with what the world needs, reveals your mission. What the world needs and what you can get paid for equals your vocation, and what you're good at, paired with what you can be paid for reveals your profession. And when all of these come together, your Ikigai is discovered.

As I mentioned earlier, finding your purpose isn't a quick process. It took me months, taking into consideration everything that I'd done in my life and everything that I wanted to achieve. Once I'd jotted down the quick and obvious things, I took the time to add a new thing every time I experienced something that felt important to me. And within this process, I also discovered that some of the 'quick and obvious' things that I initially added, weren't that important to me after all. Which is a crucial point to remember if you decide to work through this process.

We always need to be aware of our 'driving thoughts.' Very often the first things that jump to mind are the 'easy wins' but these are often the things we've tried before, and look where that has gotten us. For me, going with my first thoughts didn't always serve me well; very often because they had the negative stories that I'd told myself for years weaved throughout them. So taking your time, digging deep and getting the people you trust to help you to think things through all rate highly on my list of recommendations if you choose to do this exercise.

Finding my Ikigai, my reason for being, has been so empowering in many ways. Understanding that my purpose is to stimulate reflection, inspire belief, and ignite growth to enable myself and those around me to flourish drives me towards the things that bring me joy, happiness and enables me to feel a success in my life. Knowing my purpose helps me to keep moving forward even on the days when I wake up not feeling 'it'. And having a purpose has helped to build my resilience as now I know why I do what I do, whenever my confidence wavers or the old stories start to resurface, I remind myself of what's important to me and the difference I make to those around me which helps me to keep focused and unstuck.

Now that I've discovered this, I find my meaning in life by helping others to reflect on their challenges, to believe in themselves and the endless possibilities available to them, and to take the steps to grow into the very best versions of themselves. By having this focus I feel more fulfilled than ever before because I know that I'm adding value to other peoples' lives on a regular basis. Thus dispelling my lifelong belief that I am worthless, thick and useless.

Taking the time to reflect has been so important in understanding myself, my hopes, my dreams, my drivers, and my purpose. And now that I'm here, I am confident to share with the world who I am and what I'm all about. The brand that I ride for is filled with my personal values, my hopes for a better world, and my belief in the potential of people; especially those who may feel that they're not enough or are 'stuck' in an unhelpful moment in time.

If you are to take anything away from this chapter, please remember that if Viktor Frankl can find hope in a Nazi concentration camp, and I can view my years of sexual, physical, and psychological abuse as a series of moments to learn from (just to be clear, I don't for a second compare my experiences to Viktor Frankl's), then whatever the situation you may find yourself in whilst reading this book, hopefully you too can move forward towards finding your purpose in life that will enable you to flourish.

"The more you look for shit,
the more shit you'll find."

Steve Nestor

19. Celebrate the little wins

"You should bring something into the world that wasn't in the world before. It doesn't matter what that is. It doesn't matter if it's a table or a film, or gardening - everyone should create. You should do something, then sit back and say, 'I did that.'" Ricky Gervais

I was a housing related support worker for more than three years and during that time I worked with young parents, people leaving care, people leaving prison, those struggling with debt, and people living with mental ill health. The work that we did was paid for by the Supporting People funding stream, and as such, we needed to show the positive outcomes from our work to prove that what we were doing was worthwhile, and to help with future bids for funding for the much-needed services we offered. I obviously understand why this was needed and it was always good to be able to report that somebody had managed to clear their debts, find a job, get onto a programme to help with their drug or alcohol dependency, or was better managing their mental health but I always struggled with how the seemingly little things were overlooked when we reported outcomes.

In my experience, it's the little things that often make the biggest difference. There were loads of people who I supported who had been through the system countless times without feeling any lasting benefits from their experiences. Many of them had suffered in some way, shape or form; some had experienced childhood abuse, others were the victims of domestic violence, there were cases of Post-Traumatic Stress Disorder (PTSD). One person I supported had been a heroin addict for years following their abusive partner getting them hooked on prescription drugs before moving them on to the heavy stuff. Another was struggling to cope following their involvement in car accident that left somebody seriously injured, and a third who shared their experience of being involved in a shooting whilst being in the armed forces; a haunting experience that had seriously affected them for many years. There are lots of people who I supported that stick in my mind, but I didn't realise until writing it down just now how much the one involved in the shooting affected me.

It was during the Falklands War that the incident took place. He shot and killed a young Argentine soldier and the sound of him crying for his mother as he died had echoed around this man's mind ever since. It struck me as I was writing this passage that we'd both suffered trauma at around the same time. As I was being abused, he was experiencing the feelings that came with taking somebody's life. I never thought about it whilst I was working with him but now that I reflect, it feels right that our paths crossed when they did. Although I was there to support him, our conversations also helped me to build my empathy and my listening skills; it was tough hearing him open up about what he'd experienced and it further reinforced just how much I don't know about the lives of others and how important it is to show kindness.

There are so many people out there who have suffered a trauma of some description, many of whom are stuck in the very moment that their life changed. And this man, much like me but in very different circumstances, had been drifting through his life, replaying the terrible things that happened on that fateful day. Although he couldn't get it out of his mind, he'd spent decades denying that there was a problem and had been sweeping his emotions under the carpet with the help of alcohol. But during our sessions he began to realise that something needed to change. And once he recognised that he didn't want to live that way anymore, we set to work on creating a plan for him to move forward with his life. Over the next few months he got in touch with a charity that helped ex-military personnel, he spoke to his GP about his mental health and alcohol dependency, and he began to take responsibility for himself, and control over his life. All because he had the courage to take that first step and let me in through the front door.

As a support worker I was privileged to be allowed into many lives, and thinking about the three people that I mentioned earlier they all had very different experiences, but they all had a few things in common. None of them wanted to open the door to me when we first met. They left their letters unopened and struggled to make phone calls. They were all badly scarred by the traumas they had experienced. They couldn't see a way out, they were drowning in their negative self-thoughts and they felt unworthy of any help.

There were plenty of lessons that I learned when working with these wonderful people (and many more like them). These included the importance of being non-judgemental, the power of not giving up on people as sometimes we all need someone to believe in us, and the value of kindness. It costs nothing to listen, to show empathy, and to offer a supportive hand but it makes the world of difference to the person on the receiving end.

Another valuable lesson learned was that sometimes we just need to focus on doing the basics. We need to take the first tiny steps that will help us on the road to where we want to be. And it's the very first step that is very often the hardest one to take. Opening the door to me was a huge success for a lot of the people I supported. In some cases, I'd made several appointments with them before finally getting to the door without them cancelling. And even then, they didn't always answer, and when they did, I wasn't always invited in. Many of them had been offered help on numerous occasions before but had never felt worthy enough to take it. And being allowed into their homes was just the start.

I supported them for months, gradually building trusting relationships with them; creating a safe, non-judgemental space for them to feel comfortable enough to share their challenges and insecurities with me. During this time, they slowly faced their fears. They opened the letters that had been building up, and they braved the phone calls for the first time in years to the energy companies, rent office and debt collection agencies, and began to take responsibility for their lives.

They kept their appointments with their GPs and got the help that they needed from drug, alcohol, and mental health teams. Slowly but surely they began to gain hope that their lives could improve; that they didn't have to remain stuck in the moments that had led them to a life of pain, anguish, drugs, alcohol and depression. But without them taking that very first step, none of it would have happened. And it's so important for us all to celebrate every single win; because doing so helps to build our confidence as we begin to see that we are capable of moving forward and achieving something. And when our confidence begins to grow we begin to see possibilities. Rather than being stuck in a dark room with no windows and seemingly no way out, we begin to see blue skies and open doorways. Eventually, this increased optimism leads to us searching for opportunities because we start to learn that we are worth more than we have ever allowed ourselves to feel.

Taking the first step is usually the hardest, and often the least celebrated. Opening the door, picking up the phone, reading a letter were all huge challenges that the people I supported had to overcome before they even began to think about tackling some of the 'bigger' stuff. And for me, the first step was realising that although I thought I was okay with what happened to me as a child because I'd managed to live a relatively 'normal' life as a young adult, the fact was that I'd been sweeping my true feelings under the carpet for years. And that if I was ever to escape the chains of his words and his abuse I was going to have to put some serious work in because I realised that if you keep sweeping things under the carpet, one day you're going to trip over that pile of crap.

I've got to be honest though, I didn't realise just how hard that work would be. It would prove to be work that would challenge my thinking, challenge my definition of who I thought I was; work that would sometimes lead to me feeling frustrated and angry at my lack of progress; and work that is never, ever done. But it is worth the effort.

By taking that first step I've managed to get away (for the most part) from feeling worthless, useless and thick. Over the last 10 years or so, I graduated, moved from a support worker role into a communications and marketing position, and then onto becoming a professional coach in a Learning & Development team before being made redundant during the COVID-19 pandemic.

I'd been in my 'dream' job for around two years when the organisation I was working for went through a restructure and decided that they no longer needed our roles. Years ago I would have felt like a victim if this had happened to me, but I've worked hard to minimise that 'It's because it's me' voice in my head, and instead I saw redundancy as an opportunity to try something for myself. I was nearly 50 and had worked full-time since I was 16. I'd always fancied being my own boss but had never been brave enough to give it a go; self-employment and having your own business was something that other people did. I thought that if I didn't try it at that point, I probably never would and I'd have to live with that regret for the rest of my life.

So I set to work on my coaching and mentoring business idea. I thought of a name, designed a website, created a logo, social media accounts, email addresses, and my initial marketing campaigns. It was during this time that I worked on what my purpose is, my reason for getting out of bed in the morning. I realised that my greatest pleasure and satisfaction came from helping people to see that they didn't have to 'settle' for their lives. If something isn't working for people, if they don't feel happy, fulfilled or content, I love helping them use their past experiences to build hope and belief in themselves so that they can grow and flourish; so creating a business that would help people in this way was the obvious way for me to go. I was loving life. I managed to get a few clients that helped to pay the bills. I was being creative, meeting new people, and sharing my passion for coaching and still having time for myself. What could be better?

It turns out that I liked the idea of working for myself much more than actually doing it. I was the owner of Big Green Ears for around a year before deciding that it wasn't for me. I realised that I needed to be part of something bigger, it wasn't enough to be able to pay the bills, I needed to be around people, to be part of a team working towards a common goal, so I decided to put myself out there and see what happened. This realisation, and recognising that the reality of my situation was that I would be self-employed and chasing work for the rest of my life, working evenings and weekends when my wife was working Monday to Friday 9 to 5 helped me to take the easy decision to get back into paid employment.

I loved my time being self-employed. I learned so much about myself, my motivations, my needs, and my hopes for the future. I 'scratched' a life-long itch and can happily say that I gave it a go. And you never know, if my circumstances change, I may revisit the idea one day (never say never) but I have no plans to do so in the foreseeable future because that experience led me to taking a job with Raise the Bar as a Learning & Development Consultant, and I've never been happier. And this opportunity only came about because I decided to put myself out there and tell the world what I wanted. Understanding what my personal purpose is, realising that I needed to feel valued, be part of something bigger than me, contributing to a wider purpose, and working for an organisation that truly believes in the potential of people as much as I do, I went about creating the 'Wanted Poster' that I mentioned earlier; Cowboy style obviously, and posted it on LinkedIn.

And during my first year at Raise the Bar;

- I travelled to Australia for work
- I found a passion for apprenticeships that I never knew existed
- Developed learning experiences and delivered engaging sessions on leadership, professional coaching, and equality & diversity
- Worked with lots of incredible people, watching them grow and seeing their careers going from strength to strength
- Hosted national webinars and interviewed inspirational speakers for podcasts
- Made some great friends
- Felt valued, trusted and supported
- Been encouraged to be me.

As I write this I'm still on a high from spending time with my colleagues 'in real life' for the first time. I've been with Raise the Bar since November 2021, and until this weekend (December 2022) I'd only met one person from the organisation face to face; but we certainly put that right during our colleague conference at the gorgeous Knowsley Hall, followed by the best Christmas party ever at The Baltic Hotel in Liverpool.

During the day time we had a ceremony to celebrate and bring our company values to life, and I was so privileged to be nominated by some of my colleagues for the #WeCare award.

'We Care'

'We are here to listen, to provide the best support and experience to our team and customers.'

As I've mentioned, for a long time I've felt invisible in my life, so to be recognised by different people across the organisation as somebody who listens, who is there for others and who cares was a really special moment for me. I felt so proud to be standing in front of everyone and it confirmed that I made the right decision to get involved in something that is much bigger than me, that enables me to fulfil my purpose every single day. But if I hadn't taken the time to define my purpose, to explore how I wanted to feel (rather than what I wanted to do), I may still be 'floating' around now, waiting for something to happen to me instead of putting myself out there and taking control of my life.

It's easy to think that the world owes you something when you've not had the best time in life. I did for a long time but the fact is, if you want to change something or achieve something you have to put the work in yourself. If, like me, you find yourself in a position where things aren't working for you, put yourself out there, be your authentic self, and tell people what's important to you and what you're looking for. Who knows what opportunity is waiting for you.

"Keep being you." Luke Chapman

"Once we realise that there's more to life
than what we can see at this moment
we start to think differently.
And when we're feeling stuck,
thinking differently is good."

Steve Nestor

20. Are you in?

"Life is supposed to be fun. It's not a job or an occupation. We're only here once and we should have a bit of a laugh."
Billy Connolly

I'm not going to go into detail about the conference and Christmas party but there's a point I'd like to make here that I realise has been a crucial aspect in me being able to live a life on my terms. During the day time, we had the pleasure of the wonderful James Sills, who led 70 of us in a group singing session. A few years ago this kind of activity would have struck fear into the very heart of me, but a while ago I made a clear decision and have stuck with it ever since; and it has made such a difference to how I feel in every situation I find myself in. Whenever something is happening I ask myself a very simple question. Am I in?

If the answer is 'no', I politely walk away and don't get involved. But if the answer is 'yes' (and it very often is) then I'm 'in' completely. One hundred percent. No holding back. No feeling embarrassed. No restrictions on being myself; and do you know what? It feels amazing! I was 'in' during the singing session with James; I was 'in' when the microphone was handed to me and I had to make up a story on the spot because our table had been too busy chatting rather than doing the exercise we'd been asked to do; I was 'in' when it came to dancing at the party in the evening and I was 'in' when it came to staying up until nearly 6am chatting and laughing with colleagues.

"The tapestry of relationships can weave into a beautiful team dynamic" Paris Carey

I've learned that holding back has not served me well on the whole. Whenever I put my heart and soul into anything I do, be that friendships, work, singing, dancing, hobbies, learning, and being myself I always feel good. Whenever I've held back in the past, I've been left feeling unfulfilled, dissatisfied, and regretful. I'm not sure if it has anything to do with getting older and realising that unless I live to be over 100 I've been on this earth for longer than I've got left, but the last few years have been a revelation for me. I feel like I've stepped out of my own shadow and am finally feeling happy and successful. I'm living my life on my terms because I've realised that I only have one go at this and I want to enjoy every single minute as much as I possibly can. The past has gone, the future is still to be written, all we really have is now, this very moment in time, and I am determined to make the most of it and hope that my reflections help you make the most of your life too.

Understanding what happiness means to me, and defining what success feels like have been crucial in my quest to live a life on my terms. It's easy to think that lots of money, a fancy car, or the latest phone will bring you happiness and make you feel successful; and it may well do. I'm not here to say that it doesn't, but what I am here to do is ask you to take a little time to think about where you are, how you feel, and (this is the important bit) how you want to feel. And if there are gaps between where you are and where you want to be, consider the tiniest first step that you need to take to help you on your way to your version of happiness and success. What are you holding back on?

I went off on a bit of a tangent there (I told you that I talk / write to think) so I'd like to rewind a little and go back a few paragraphs to the previous chapter when I said, *'...that experience led me to taking a job with Raise the Bar...'* This implies that it was only the time working for myself that gave me the opportunity. In fact, the opportunity was created way back when (nearly 20 years earlier) I decided that I wasn't going to settle for being a shell of a person, living in the shadow of my abusive years.

Every single step that I've taken has led me to this point in my life, but there is one moment in particular that stands out in my mind. It's nothing ground-breaking but it was the first time that I remember ever setting a clear goal for myself. It was 2009 and I was working as a sales executive (fancy job title, crap job selling advertising space in a local newspaper) and was really unhappy. I'd been there for around three years and kept telling myself that it was okay. It paid the bills, it was secure, I had a company car, it was local, the people I worked with were nice. But when it got to the point that I dreaded Monday morning as I was leaving work on a Friday evening I knew something had to change. So on Wednesday the 23rd September 2009 I sat at my desk and declared to my colleagues that I would find a new job by 23rd October (just over four weeks away). I circled the date on my desk-top calendar and immediately felt empowered.

I'd been moaning about my job for ages, hating the evenings and weekends because all I could think about was how I didn't want to go to work. I was getting lower and lower because I felt stuck, but by making the decision to take action and setting myself a deadline I suddenly discovered a new lease of life and set to work searching through the jobs pages. Within days I saw it. A job as a housing related support worker for a housing association. The money was less and there was no company car but the role looked like something that I'd enjoy. As always, Tracy was so supportive as a drop in wage and buying a car shouldn't have been an option at the time as we were pretty skint, but she could see how unhappy I was and so she encouraged me to go for it. I completed the application, attended an assessment centre with fellow candidates, got invited back for an interview and was subsequently offered the job. And I handed my notice in to the newspaper on 23 October 2009.

On reflection, I realise that until I took the job as support worker, I'd never been 'in' with any role that I'd ever had - they were always a means to an end, there was no emotion attached to them, my heart and soul were never in them. I'd never felt worthy of pursuing a career so I'd jumped from job to job; careers were for people who went to college and university; not for 'thick' people like me who left school with just two 'O' Levels. But being offered the support worker role changed something inside me. I was suddenly doing something worthwhile, something that added value to other peoples' lives, something that helped me feel like maybe, just maybe, I wasn't worthless and useless after all. I didn't realise it at the time, but that job would be a huge factor in me discovering my purpose in life and would lead me to feeling how I feel today.

21. Life isn't a straight line

"Change is the only constant." Astrid Purnomo

Although there's no denying that we get older every day, and that the steps we take (or don't take) influence the life that we live, in my experience, there's no guarantee that just because we move 'past' something in our lives that we can put it to bed and forget about it. For years I tried to push my experiences to the back of my mind and just get on with things. I told myself that it was history, and that I was a product of my past and to accept that it was just way it was so there was no point even thinking about it.

In reality though, my past was never far from the front of mind. I blamed it for everything, and even when I started to think differently about things it was always nagging away at me. Reminding me that I was worthless and useless whenever I thought about trying something new. When I met Tracy I struggled to believe that she liked me and to accept that she wanted to be with me. In the early days of our relationship I was so jealous of her past, constantly comparing myself to what I knew of her past boyfriends, which inevitably led to a number of fiery arguments which in turn, fuelled my insecurities. Why would she want to be with a loser like me? I was honest with Tracy about my actions that led to the ending of my first marriage from very early on and it was definitely the right thing to do; but at the time it felt like another nail in my coffin. Why would she want to be with someone who hadn't been faithful in a marriage? What a catch I was. On reflection Tracy never made me feel this way, I was projecting my negative self-thoughts onto her. For some reason that I don't completely understand (remember I said that I'm not a therapist) I wanted to cause trouble between us. Why would I do that? We were in a new relationship, we really liked each other, we were having a lot of fun together, and had loads in common; I suppose it all comes back to me feeling like I didn't deserve any of it.

Luckily for me, Tracy could see something in me that I never saw in myself and helped me to work through what was going on for me. She didn't take any crap from me and would always stand up for herself in any argument or disagreement that we had; in fact, thinking about it, I don't think I've actually 'won' an argument with her in all the time we've been together. Importantly Tracy didn't only not take any crap from me, she challenged my thinking, helping me to begin to explore why I thought I wasn't worthy, and supported me in thinking through the negative language she noticed that I was using about myself.

She helped me to see that my past didn't have to define my present and my future. We talked, cried and most powerfully, laughed a lot about my past.

Laughing about my abusive childhood might sound like a strange thing to do but it worked for me, which is not that surprising as comedy has always been my go to as an escape. I like music but have never had a favourite band or genre. I can listen to anything depending on my mood. In the last week alone Alexa has been asked to play Guns 'n' Roses, Adele, Oasis, Sam Fender, Pink, The Killers, Tears for Fears, Coldplay, Ed Sheeran, John Lennon, Boy George, Robbie Williams, Texas, Queen, Alanis Morissette, Tom Grennan, James, Paulo Nutini, Neil Diamond, Jamiroquai (love a bit of Space Cowboy), a spot of Northern Soul, and a bit of classical piano for good measure. I've never been able to 'escape' when listening to music, my mind always seems to wander and if I'm not careful I can end up thinking (often unhealthily) about the things that weren't good in my life. But comedy has always helped. I remember watching the likes of Kelly Monteith, Dave Allen, Spike Milligan, The Two Ronnies, Cannon and Ball, Russ Abbott, Monty Python, and The Young Ones, and losing myself in their worlds. As time has gone on, Ben Elton, Eddie Izzard, Rhod Gilbert, Vic Reeves, Lee Mack, Sean Lock, Lee Evans, Ricky Gervais, and the one and only Billy Connolly (amongst many others) have all been there when I need a laugh to take my mind off things. I've been guilty of taking myself too seriously in the past, and laughing with Tracy helped me step back from what had happened to me and see it from a different perspective. Which led me to recognise that what has gone has gone, but the lessons from our experiences are always there to be learned from, and laughed at if that helps.

My reflections have shown me that although I'm making progress and am definitely on the right tracks, I still have my fair share of moments when I experience self-doubt and am not very kind to myself. But do you know what, I've accepted that's how it will probably be for the rest of my life and I'm okay with that. I've realised that I need to deal with facts and no matter how much I say that I shouldn't talk negatively to myself, that I need to believe in myself more and that I can live a life on my terms, it is unrealistic to expect to go through every day for the rest of my life without any doubts at all. What I experienced changed me from the person that I could have been into the person that I have been, and it will always be a part of who I am. And to deny that would be to deny myself of all the things I experienced and everything that I've learned about myself over the years.

Also, to expect to never have those deep-rooted beliefs and thoughts surface once in a while would feel like I was setting myself up to fail. I need to be prepared, I need to deal with the reality that this stuff is a bit like herpes in so much as it might go away for a while, it might not surface very often, it may lie dormant, but it's always there and it never, ever leaves you, (by the way, I just want to make it clear that I don't have herpes). Having this knowledge and keeping things 'real' helps me to notice my old thinking patterns and take steps to deal with them as early as possible to stop them returning me to a place that I really don't want to go back to.

By taking time (lots of it) to understand myself and define how I want to feel in my life, I've found ways to put my doubts and negative self-talk into perspective. I can't remember the last time I blamed my past for how I'm feeling in the present. I now take full responsibility for my emotions and by doing so, I feel completely in control.

This way of thinking was massively helped when I was studying for my degree. One of the six modules I chose was an introduction to six major religions which I took purely because I had very little knowledge of religious beliefs and was curious to find out more. During my studies, comparisons were made between the linear nature of Christianity; we're born, we live, we learn, we die, we go to heaven (or not), the end, and religions such as Hinduism, Sikhism and Buddhism where life is seen as a cycle. We're born, we live, we learn, we die, we're reborn, we live, we learn, we die, we're reborn until we reach the ultimate heights of Moksha or Nirvana. In other words, we're continually learning, growing and becoming enlightened until we're freed from ignorance, liberated from suffering attached to our worldly existence, and find the highest form of happiness. Just to say, I only lightly touched on these ideas during my studies so please accept my apologies if my interpretations don't match your reality.

Since reading about these ideas I've not converted to any kind of religion but my thinking around how I live my life was hugely influenced. It brought it home to me that life isn't a straight line; I'm not sure that I believe in reincarnation, I'm not sure that I don't believe in it either, but I know for sure that if I only have this one life, I want to make the absolute most of it. And believing that we are here to learn (whether in this life or any subsequent ones we may be granted) has helped me put my experiences into perspective and to use them for good. We're surrounded by sayings like 'life begins at 40' but I don't find this way of thinking very helpful at all. It feeds into the idea that as we get older, everything will be okay. As we work through our lives, all will fall into place; but how helpful is that to those of us who have deep-rooted feelings of worthlessness that will never completely go away. I've found that a more helpful way of living is to accept what has happened, to take what we need from the experience, to believe that our lives are filled with opportunities if we take the time to recognise them, and use those experiences and opportunities to grow into the very best version of ourselves.

"Looking up helps me to believe that there is a Universe of possibilities out there to explore and discover; as long as I don't get lost in my own head."

Steve Nestor

22. Your future is still unwritten

"What's meant for you won't pass you by." Jacqui Mortimer

Hopefully I've shown through my reflections that every single one of us has the power to decide how we'd like to respond to the events of our lives. My experiences have proved to me that we are not stuck in any moment. Situations pass and, if we look for them, there are lessons in everything that happens around us. We all have the potential to live a life on our terms, a life that brings our very own versions of happiness, fulfilment, success, meaning and purpose if we only believe in ourselves and commit to take the actions that will point us in the right direction. I've learned that there will be disappointment in life and things won't go to plan every time, so the sooner we understand that we always have the opportunity to learn and take a different path, the sooner we take control and become unstuck.

Please believe that every moment you get the opportunity to choose what comes next, as my good friend Jacqui Mortimer would say; "I decide…"

What do you want? How do you want to feel? Who do you want to be? The power is yours to decide.

Now that I've shared my reflections, I'd like to show you some simple, but effective exercises (some of which I have created) that have helped me. My hope is that, if you need them, they might help you through any challenges you may be facing too. Very often I've found that using a single tool or exercise isn't enough to achieve what I've been hoping to, so I find myself mixing and matching exercises and ideas and creating my own so I gain the most benefit. For example, when discovering my purpose I started by using the concept of Ikigai to get an idea of what I love doing, what I'm good at, what the world needs more of, and how I could add value to myself and those around me, and then combined it with elements of my version of the Cowboy Code and my Reflect, Believe, Grow model to help me to create something unique to me that I could use to help me to live a life on my terms.

As I said at the beginning of the book, this is my story but it is all about you. So please take what you need from the following ideas and make them your own.

Start from where you are

Once we know where we are we can then decide where we want to be and the steps we need to take to get there. Answer these questions to help to build your self-awareness and decide what living a life on your terms means for you.

- How are you feeling?
- What is important to you?
- Why is that so important?
- Who is important to you?
- What is good in your life?
- What would you like more of in your life?
- What prompted you to read this book?
- If money was no object, how would you spend your days?
- What are you putting up with?
- What is holding you back?
- If you had more time what would you do?
- What are your hopes and dreams?
- What are your strengths, skills and talents?
- When are you at your happiest?
- What are you most proud of?
- How committed are you to making a change?

As with all of the questions and exercises in this book, please think through your answers, take your time, and be completely honest with yourself.

CAMP

All of the things that I have done (and continue to do) come from the belief that I have the power to choose to experience something in a different way. Once I'd realised that, I started layering tools and techniques on top of this idea. One of the most effective 'models' that I've created for myself is CAMP.

As most cowboys seem to like a good camp fire, the idea is to use the CAMP framework as a basis for a good old fashioned conversation; either with yourself or those you trust. Turn off all distractions and imagine yourself in the Old West. No phones, emails, TVs, games consoles or computers, just the warmth of the campfire, some bacon and beans warming through, and your trusty horse for company. Work with this framework to reframe the situation you find yourself in. What might you need to change?

C is for Chatter. I've talked a lot about negative self-talk throughout the book. Listen to how you're talking to yourself and ask how helpful and empowering it is. Would you speak to a friend the same way you speak to yourself? If your self-talk is not serving you well, commit to changing. Be kind to yourself.

A is for Attention. Where is your focus? Remember that wherever your attention is, that is where your energy will flow to. If you're looking for shit, you'll keep finding shit. Shift your focus towards the positive. Stop thinking about what has gone wrong, and how you don't want to feel, and begin to open your mind to the possibilities that are out there and set goals and work towards them. This will help you feel the way you want to feel and lead you to living a life on your terms.

M is for Movement. When you feel stuck, physically moving around can have a huge impact on your mood. I often move from room to room, go for a walk, put on some music, listen to comedy, or stand outside 'looking up' to help shift my emotions from negative and disempowering ones, to those where I feel positive and can see possibilities instead of dead-ends.

P is for Perspective. I was 'stuck' for a long time because I didn't open my mind to thinking differently. I only saw the world through my very narrow, tainted, window on it. Whatever you're going through (or have gone through) challenge yourself to see it from a different angle. What other more helpful meanings and perspectives can you put to your experiences? How else might you see it? What different perspective can you give to it that will help you move forward?

Five senses

If you find yourself feeling stressed, anxious, or overwhelmed, the five senses exercise is an effective way to hit the 'stop' button in your mind and bring yourself back to the present moment. All you need to do is to stop thinking and focus on:

5 things you can see. Look for the detail within things. The trick is to take your mind off your current worries, so take your time.

4 things you can hear. What distant sounds can you pick up when you really listen?

3 things you can feel. Take the time to notice and explore the texture of the objects around you.

2 things you can smell. Take a deep breath in through your nose. What aromas can you sense? This one is a little tricky for me as I have no sense of smell so I imagine what a couple of the things that I can see, hear or feel might smell like.

1 thing you can taste. What lingering flavour do you have in your mouth?

This simple exercise helps to calm your mind and ground you back in the present moment. Putting time and space between you and your immediate worries gives you the opportunity to decide how you'd like to respond (instead of react) to whatever you may be facing.

Set goals for yourself and think them through

Goals link us from where we are now to our future. They help to turn our hopes and dreams into reality. Once you've established what you want and how you want to feel, the next step is to take action. As I've mentioned I floated through life until September 2009 when I set my first goal for myself. Since then I've made a conscious effort to set realistic targets for myself to help me achieve the things that are important to me, including writing this book. In January 2022 I wrote myself a letter using FutureMe[16] to be delivered back to me in January 2023. Within there I had set myself a target of writing the first draft of my book by the end of 2022, which I have achieved. My next steps were to edit, fine tune and publish by May 2023.

Goal setting:

- Gives us direction and a sense of purpose, helping us to find meaning
- Brings structure and gives us a sense of control over our daily lives
- Helps us to understand what's important to us
- Brings clarity and helps us to prioritise our time and efforts
- Boosts our confidence and gives us a sense of achievement

- Gives us something to work towards, to focus on, and to look forward to
- Provides anticipation and joy.

When setting goals it's important to think through a few things to ensure that it's the right goal for you and that you are completely committed to it. Without doing this first there's a good chance that you might not achieve what you hope (or even take those first, crucial steps) which could leave you feeling more 'stuck' than ever. I use the well-formed outcomes method for setting goals as it helps me to cover all bases and ensures that what I'm working on is as important to me as I first think it is. For example, when I was made redundant and started my own business I didn't really think it through. I was excited about the opportunity, and don't regret it for a second as it helped me to learn so much about myself, but I didn't consider everything that I would have to give up, and how prepared I was to do that. It was only when I was working for myself that I realised that I'd have to give up security of income, my evenings and weekends, time with my wife, and being part of something bigger, which were the main reasons why I decided that being self-employed wasn't for me at that time; leading to me setting a new goal of finding full-time employment again.

Sometimes we think we want something and jump into action only to later realise that we didn't actually want it at all. Maybe it's linked to those stories we've been telling ourselves that we haven't challenged or updated in years. Using this method helps us to think through our goals before committing to action. Here are a few things to think about, and questions to ask yourself when you're setting any goals.

1. Set your goal in positive terms

- What do you want? (not what you want to get away from/not want).

2. Identify why this is important to you.

- What will it mean for you when you achieve it, and why is that so important?

3. Make your goal sensory specific.

When we visualise how it will be for us when we've achieved our goal we have something tangible to aim for. Noticing when things start shifting in a positive direction gives us the opportunity to celebrate the little wins, helping to maintain motivation until we have reached our goal. Imagine you've achieved your goal:

- What can you see? What/who is around you?

- What can you hear? What are you saying to yourself? What are others saying to you and about you?

- How does it feel?

4. Make sure the goal is within your control.

- Do you have the resources, skills and abilities to reach this goal?

- Who else could help you?

- What steps will you need to take to achieve this?

5. Explore how reaching this goal will affect your life?

- What will achieving this goal bring to your life?

- What will you have to give up?

- How prepared and committed are you to doing that?

- How do you know that working towards this goal is a good use of your time?

6. Set a timescale

- When will you achieve your goal?

- How will you keep yourself motivated and on track?

- Who might hold you to account for your actions?

7. Test your commitment

- On a scale of 1-10 (1 being 'it's not happening') ask yourself how committed you are to this action?

- 1,2,3 or 4

- Ask yourself; Is this the right action for you at this time?

-5,6 or 7

- What needs to happen to make your score an 8,9, or 10? What do you need to do, or stop doing?

-8,9, or 10

- What will you do first?

- When exactly will you do it?

- What might get in your way?

- How will you handle it?

Following these steps and answering the questions honestly and thoroughly isn't guaranteed to bring you success, but it will, in my experience, give you a much better chance of understanding what is important to you and will set you on the right path to achieving it.

"If you keep sweeping things under the carpet, one day you're going to trip over that pile of crap."

Steve Nestor

Build your ability to bounce back

Consider this for a second; whatever you have been through in life has brought you to this moment. You got through it and are here, reading this book and working towards building a life on your terms. Now think about one of the biggest challenges you've been through and, using my Reflect, Believe and Grow model, answer the following questions.

Reflect; On your challenges and successes

- How did you get through the challenge?
- What were the first steps you took?
- What did you do?
- Who helped you?
- How might you use this knowledge to help you to move forward?

Believe; In endless possibilities

- How good does it feel to know that you have come through it?
- How has the experience changed you?
- What have you learned about yourself?
- What strengths do you recognise in yourself?
- What possibilities might be open to you if you believe in yourself a little more than you do today?

Grow; Into the very best version of you

- How can you use what you've learned about yourself to help you to overcome any present or future challenges?
- What else can you do now that you know about your strengths?
- How can you build on your strengths?
- What other strengths could you develop?

Build on your strengths

We all have skills, talents and strengths but often we don't believe in ourselves, focus on the negatives, or get stuck in the stories we tell ourselves. To combat this and to break free from our often self-imposed restraints we need to remind ourselves of all that is good in our lives. A simple way to start to change the way we think about ourselves is to make three lists and add to them whenever something new comes to mind.

1. I'm good at...

2. My friends, family and colleagues say I'm good at...

3. To build on what I'm good at, I will...

Reflect on your answers and add to them regularly and set yourself goals to help you to move towards living a life on your terms. The key to all of this is being committed to whatever the change is that you'd like to make, and to take action and actually do something about it.

If you're feeling stressed, anxious, or overwhelmed write down everything that is contributing to you feeling that way. Once you've emptied your mind, ask yourself these questions, or if you have somebody you trust and feel comfortable with, get them to ask you. It's important to be honest with yourself when answering any self-reflection questions.

- What happened to make me feel this way?
- Why did that trigger these feelings?
- When was the last time I felt this way?
- How did I handle it?
- What did I learn?
- How might I use that in this situation?
- Who helped me?
- Who could help me now?
- What would I say to somebody else in this situation?
- How much of how I'm feeling is based on fact?
- How else could I think about this?
- What do I have control over?
- What do I have to accept?
- How can I 'reset' myself?
- What would make me feel better right now?

- If I'm saying 'yes' to this, what am I saying 'no' to?

When you have taken the time to answer these questions honestly, think about what you can start, and/or stop doing to help you take control of your emotions. Think small to make the change achievable and sustainable. If we set our sights too high there's a chance that we'll feel discouraged and lose motivation so consider what you could do that would reduce your stress, anxiety, or feelings of overwhelm by just one per cent; and build on it daily to create new, more empowering, thoughts and habits.

Some things can't be changed

Accepting what you can't change, and focusing on what you can is key to helping to build resilience. We often worry about the things we can do nothing about which can drain our energy levels, often leading to feelings of overwhelm.

Make four lists:

- List 1: Write down everything that you are worried or concerned about.
- List 2: Write down what you have no control or influence over.
- List 3: Write down what you do have control or influence over.
- List 4: Now choose at least one of the things from list 3 and consider what you'd like to do about it; planning how you will do it, and when you will do it by.

Focusing on what we can control helps us to use our strengths, build confidence and resilience, and contributes to creating a positive mindset where we look for possibilities instead of problems. Something that is crucial if we are to become, and remain, unstuck.

What's important now?

"Multitasking divides your attention and leads to confusion and weakened focus." Deepak Chopra

Multitasking is sold as something that we should all be good at, we're told that we need to multitask to be efficient and successful. Busyness is often worn as a badge of honour, but in truth when we attempt to juggle important tasks most of us are challenging our brains in ways that could lead to us feeling overwhelmed. Let me show you what I mean with a little, fun exercise. You'll need a piece of paper, a pen or pencil, and something to time yourself with, maybe your stopwatch on your mobile phone.

1. Start your stopwatch and write the sentence and numbers as shown below. Then stop your stopwatch and make a note of your time;

I think cowboys are great

1 2 3 4 5 6 7 8 9 10 11 12 13 14 15 16 17 18 19 20 21

2. Reset your stopwatch and play some music, or switch on the TV and then write the same thing again. But this time you'll need to alternate between letters and numbers.

So, start with I, then write 1, Then it will be 't', followed by 2, then 'h' followed by 3... and so on until you reach the end. Once finished, stop your stopwatch and make a note of your time.

Now answer these questions;

1. What is the time difference between your first and second attempts?

2. How many mistakes did you make the second time?

3. How did you feel the second time compared to the first?

The purpose of this bit of fun is to show that most of us can't multitask. As with everything in life there are exceptions, but most people that I've done this exercise with take longer the second time around (often double the time), they tend to make more mistakes, and often say that they put pressure on themselves second time round and start to feel a little stressed.

This is because we are switching between tasks and our brains have to stop and restart the thinking process when we're being forced to think in different ways and focus on more than one thing. This suggests that trying to focus on multiple things at the same time can lead to feelings of overwhelm, potentially leading to longer completion times and resulting in us making mistakes. This can lead to feeling stressed and may knock our confidence, eat away at our resilience, and possibly reinforce those unhelpful stories we've been telling ourselves, which ultimately keep us 'stuck.'

Once we decide what the most important thing to do is, everything else becomes unimportant.

Remember earlier in the book when I said that we only really have this moment, well, keep that in mind whenever your attention and energies are being pulled in different directions. Once we decide what actions we're going to take to help us become unstuck we need to focus on what the most important action is that we need to take and remove all distractions to give ourselves the best possible chance of success.

I've mentioned that I love to keep things simple and the realisation that I wasn't moving forward because I was trying to do too many things at once and often getting nowhere, was a revelation in my personal progress. By thinking about what is important to me in any given moment I've been able to focus on the things that make a real difference. And these things come in all shapes and sizes. Sometimes it's as simple as recognising that it is important that I take time for a break or to eat (and enjoy) my breakfast with no distractions, including leaving my phone where I can't check it. Other times I have turned off email, social media and other notifications so I can concentrate on tasks that I need to get done. Writing this book is a good example. When I first started I was constantly distracted by the TV and social media but after a couple of months of not making much progress I took my own advice and removed all distractions whenever I decided that writing was the most important thing for me to do at that time.

What's taking your attention away from the things that are important to you? Make a list of what you want to achieve and the things that are getting your way. How will you ensure that you set the time aside to help you move forward with the things that are important now?

Ikigai

I've talked about how finding my purpose has been an important part of me being able to live a life on my terms and mentioned earlier in the book how discovering the concept of Ikigai has helped me to do that. If this is something that you think you'd find helpful, here are a few questions to help you to start to explore what your Ikigai might be;

What do I love?

- What is your passion?
- What do you never get bored of?
- What makes you smile?
- When do you feel at your happiest?
- What were you doing when you last lost track of time?
- If you were financially secure, what would you do with your time?
- If you could be the best at one thing, what would it be?
- What excites you?
- What could you talk about for hours on end?

What am I good at?

- What is your vocation?
- What do people approach you for help with?
- What skills do you list on your CV?

- If you had to teach something, what would it be?
- What do other people compliment you about?
- What achievements are you proud of?
- What parts of your current job come easily to you?

What does the world need?

- What is your mission?
- How can you contribute positively to those around you?
- What changes would you like to bring about in the world or your community?
- What can you offer that would bring meaning to others?
- How do you help others?
- What can you teach others?

What can I get paid for?

- What could your profession be?
- What would you be doing if you weren't in your current job?
- What have you been paid for before?
- What do other people get paid for doing?
- Are people willing to pay for what you can offer?

Please remember that these questions are simply prompts to get you started. Finding your Ikigai or purpose is something that will take time and effort. As with most things that are worth having, it takes patience and a real commitment from you. But I can say with hand on heart that from my experience, it's been the most worthwhile exercise that I've ever done. Finding my purpose helps me to stay unstuck. It drives me to get involved in things that really mean something to me, and it guides me towards ensuring that each and every day I do something that makes me feel valuable, visible, useful and worthy.

What are you grateful for?

If you find yourself focusing your attention on what you don't have, or you listen to your negative self-talk more than is helpful, thinking about what you are grateful for helps to focus the mind on what is good in your life and what you value. Practising gratitude helps to build self-awareness, resilience, and a positive, optimistic mindset. It's easy to focus on the negatives, the things we don't have, and the things that haven't gone to plan; especially in challenging times and when we feel stuck. Take a few moments each day to think about what you are grateful for and what brought a smile to your face today.

Who inspires you and why?

I've talked about the impact that my wife and Billy Connolly have had on me, but who inspires you and why? Think about the people you admire and consider how 'adding' a few of their traits to your life might help you to live a life on your terms.

A few more questions to ask yourself.

This book is designed to help anybody who is feeling 'stuck' so it's only right that I add a few more self-reflection questions that might help you move forward.

- Where would I like to be?
- When I'm in that place, how does it feel? What can I see?
- When I'm there, what are people saying, and what am I saying to myself?
- How else could I look at this situation?
- How would somebody I trust look at this situation?
- What do I actually have control over?
- What can be changed?
- How might I change the way I feel about this situation?
- How can I be kind to myself in this situation?
- What would I say to somebody else in the same situation?
- What are the facts here?
- What is the real challenge for me?
- How committed to moving forward am I?
- What is the first, tiny step that I could take?

23. Everybody needs a Mrs Nestor

" I always have time for people."
Jo Mason

Everybody needs somebody to believe in them, and if you feel that you don't at this point in your life, then please be the one who offers the support to someone who needs it.

I realised that I needed to be believed in and valued, and to feel part of something bigger than just me. I needed something more than settling for an existence on the treadmill of life. I have to believe that that I'm contributing and adding good to the world. I know now that I've always had it in me to be more than I was but without the support and belief of Mrs Nestor, I'm not sure I would have taken the steps that I have.

If you can relate to anything I've shared in this book you may fall into one of two camps. And whichever it is please consider taking action to help either yourself or those around you. If you need help, reach out. Share your thoughts and story, talk to people, don't be alone, believe that you are valuable and precious.

If you know someone who needs help, please be kind, don't judge, ask what they need, listen to them, spend time with them and be a friend. Be the one who believes in them. Be their Mrs Nestor. Who knows what a difference you might make.

"I've learned that people will forget what you said, people will forget what you did, but people will never forget how you made them feel." Maya Angelou

What next?

I've written this book in the hope that my experiences and reflections will give you a little boost and act as a friendly hand on your shoulder if and when you need it. I truly believe that we all have the potential to flourish and to live a life on our terms if we only give ourselves a chance. I've realised that I stood in my own way for a very long time and it was only when I started thinking in terms of what I wanted and how I wanted to feel, that things started to change. I started setting goals for myself and worked on re-writing the unhelpful stories I'd been telling myself into empowering ones based on truth and reality that helped my confidence and self-worth to grow. I started to believe in myself, and to believe that I was actually worthy of feeling happy and content.

As I've said throughout this book, I am a work in progress. But because of my shift in mindset, the commitment I have towards living my purpose, achieving my goals, my ongoing self-development, and my belief that we can use any experience to help us to move toward living a life on our terms, I've worked out how to become unstuck. And because of this, every day I'm building from a stronger foundation than the day before.

"You can't go back and change the beginning, but you can start where you are and change the ending." C.S. Lewis

Acknowledgments:

There's a phrase that originates from an African proverb that says;

'It takes a village to raise a child"

Although I'm not a child any more, each and every one of the following people have helped me to grow, develop and flourish. And without their love, support, belief, honest feedback, friendship, kindness or inspiration this book would never have made it out of my head, onto the paper, and now into your life. I want you to know that I'll be forever grateful to each and every one of you for the times our paths have crossed and the impact you have had on me.

Aimee Bateman, Aimee Birch, Alex Green (Abbotts), Alex Bird, Alexia Diver, Ali Dewji, Alison Short, Amanda Stearn, Amy Brann, Andreanna Dais-Patterson, Andy Johnson, Andy Parton, Angela Blanchard, Anna Walsh, Annabel Wise, Arthur Malkin, Astrid Purnomo, Ayo Sokale, Becs Bridge, Ben Smith, Bennett Taracena, Billy Connolly, Charlotte Aspley, Charlotte Fotherby, Cheryl Stevens, Cheryl Sutcliffe, Clare Johns, Clare Paterson, Danielle Bowater, Dave Cooper, Dave Green, Debby Cooper, Dominique Zacharzewski, Donna Fraser, Donna Reid, Elaine Palmer, Ele George, Ellie Cronshaw, Ellie Gooch, Elliot Newton, Epiphany Kidd, Gemma Holder, George Anderson, Georgia

Parker, Hannah Broadhead, Hayley Grainger, Hazel O'Halloran, Howard Jones, Imogen Lewis, James Sills, James Walsh, Jamil Qureshi, Janette Healey, Jacqui Mortimer, Jayme Rubenstein, Jill Lewis, Jo Mason, Jo Thackwray, Jo Wright, John Wade, Jonathan Stanger, Jordan Diver, Joseph Fallone, Julie Moseley, Katie Malone, Kelly Jefferies, Kelly Joynes, Kelly Wickens, Kenny Palmer, Kerry Tonks, Kim Bethell, Kira Burrows, Kirsty Darby, Laura King, Lauren Healey, Leanne Logan, Leila Green, Les Green, Lisa Lippett, Lucy Jones, Luisa Hatcher, Luke Chapman, Luke Palmer, Marie Church, Mary Regan, Melissa Sterling, Michelle Grocott, Michelle Mayer, Mick Kent, Moreen Pascal, My sister and brother-in-law, Natalie Halldron, Nic Hamilton, Nick Cummins, Nicole Foster, Nikki Link, Paris Carey, Parul Gupta, Paul Tran, Paula Richards, Philippa Jones, Pooja Thacoor, Poonam Veja, Rebecca Winn, Richard Lockley, Rob Wickens, Robert Bowers, Rosanna Mastropaolo, Rosie Williams, Rucha Roberts, Sam Siviter, Sharon Lockley, Shaun Lanceley, Sophia Clemmer, Steve Barnes, Steve Smith, Sue Penny, Sureka Garg, Susan Bowell, Suzanne Shead, Stu Bailey, Tim Campbell, Tim Roberts, Tim West, Toni Stephenson, Victoria Etchells, Vikki Mack, Warren Thomas, Wendy Aronson, Wendy Stephens, Zakaria Boumliha, and Zoe Jepson.

Thank you all for being such important members of my village, you'll always have a special place in my heart.

Extra help and support

If you have been affected by anything shared please get in touch with the relevant professionals so that you get the help that you deserve. There are lots of organisations and charities out there doing fabulous work that you might find helpful to contact, including:

NSPCC: https://www.nspcc.org.uk/

Childline: https://www.childline.org.uk/

Sexual Abuse Support Campaign:
https://sexualabusesupport.campaign.gov.uk/

The Samaritans: https://www.samaritans.org/

Safeline: https://safeline.org.uk/

The Survivors Trust: https://www.thesurvivorstrust.org/

Rape Crisis: https://rapecrisis.org.uk/

SARAS: https://www.sarsas.org.uk/

NAPAC: https://napac.org.uk/

1 in 6: https://www.1in6.uk/

Into the light: https://www.intothelight.org.uk/

Link to find extra support via Into the Light: https://www.intothelight.org.uk/finding-support-sexual-abuse-support/

Male Survivors Partnership: https://malesurvivor.co.uk/

Links to a directory of services via Male Survivors Partnership: https://malesurvivor.co.uk/support-for-male-survivors/directory-of-services/

Men and Boys Coalition: https://www.menandboyscoalition.org.uk/

Survivors UK: https://www.survivorsuk.org/

*All of these websites were last accessed on 21 April 2023.

References:

1. Wise, R. (1965). *The Sound of Music.* Twentieth Century Fox.

2. Code of the West. Center for Cowboy Ethics and Leadership. Available at https://cowboyethics.org/cowboy-ethics/ (Last accessed 18 March 2023)

3. The GROW Model. Sir John Whitmore and Performance Consultants. Available at https://www.performanceconsultants.com/grow-model (Last accessed 18 March 2023)

4. *I am the one and only.* Sung by Chesney Hawkes
Written by: Nik Kershaw
Lyrics © BMG Rights Management, Universal Music Publishing Group, Sony/ATV Music Publishing LLC
Lyrics Licensed & Provided by LyricFind

5. Haig, Matt. (2015). *Reasons to Stay Alive.* Canongate Books Ltd.

6. Childline. Available at https://www.childline.org.uk/ (Last accessed 18 March 2023)

7. Mitchell, Wendy. *Somebody I used to know.* Read by Rachel Atkins, Published by Bolinda / Audible audio. Released 1 June 2018

8. Definition of ***survivor noun*** from the Oxford Advanced Learner's Dictionary Available at https://www.oxfordlearnersdictionaries.com/definition/english/survivor (Last accessed 18 March 2023).

9.Young Minds. Understanding trauma and adversity.

Available at https://www.youngminds.org.uk/professional/resources/understanding-trauma-and-adversity/ (Last accessed 18 March 2023)

10. Manchester University NHS Foundation Trust (MFT). Adverse Childhood Experiences (ACEs) and Attachment. Available at https://mft.nhs.uk/rmch/services/camhs/young-people/adverse-childhood-experiences-aces-and-attachment/ (Last accessed 18 March 2023

11. Allana Cooks-Campbell. How to use the emotion wheel to get to know yourself (April 2022) Available at https://www.betterup.com/blog/emotion-wheel (Last accessed 18 March 2023)

12. *Read all about it (PtIII)*
Songwriters: Adele Emily Sande / Benjamin Alexander Kohn / Iain James / Peter Kelleher / Stephen Manderson / Thomas Andrew Searle Barnes

Read All About It, Pt. III lyrics © Bucks Music Group, Sony/ATV Music Publishing LLC, The Royalty Network Inc., Warner Chappell Music, Inc

13. From Wikipedia, the free encyclopedia. Nestor (Mythology) Available at https://en.wikipedia.org/wiki/Nestor_(mythology) (Last accessed 18 March 2023)

14. Frankl, Viktor E. *Man's Search for Meaning. The classic tribute to hope from the Holocaust.* (2004) Rider, an imprint of Ebury Publishing. Random House Group.

15. Garcia, Hector and Miralles, Fransesc. *Ikigai. The Japanese Secret to a Long and Happy Life.'* (2016) Hutchinson. Penguin Random House.

16. FutureMe. Write a letter to your future self. Available at https://www.futureme.org/ (Last accessed 18 March 2023)

Printed in Great Britain
by Amazon

35951681R00156